Praise for *Cat Call*

"Kristen Sollée flips the catcall on itself by dismantling patriarchal uses of the feline to discredit the intimidating power of the pussy while gifting us with a book that leaves you eager to embrace your personal cat power."

—**Sophie Saint Thomas**, sex writer, witch, and author of *Finding Your Higher Self: Your Guide to Cannabis for Self-Care*

"*Cat Call* is *the* necessary text that links the feline, the feminine, and the magical. In many ways, it's the cat lover's modern epic poem, an ode to the many sacred archetypes we can all tap into—the feral, the fear-inducing, the autonomous. From Venice's "kitten-carrying drag queens" to the necromancer cat of Japan, Sollée treats her readers to the delicious mythos of the cat, with meticulous research and gorgeous prose. For any cat lover or witch, this book is a feverish examination of the feline in our dreams and in our lives—and within ourselves. Page by page, you'll tap into your most catty, feral, transgressive self— caught with the delicious story of the cat between your claws."

—**Lisa Marie Basile**, author of *Light Magic for Dark Times* and *Wordcraft Witchery*

CAT CALL

Reclaiming the Feral Feminine

KRISTEN J. SOLLÉE

foreword by Pam Grossman

**WEISER
BOOKS**

This edition first published in 2019 by Weiser Books, an imprint of
Red Wheel/Weiser, LLC
With offices at:
65 Parker Street, Suite 7
Newburyport, MA 01950
www.redwheelweiser.com

ISBN: 978-1-57863-662-4
Library of Congress Cataloging-in-Publication Data available upon request.

Cover art and design by Kathryn Sky-Peck
Typography by Kasandra Cook
Typeset in Sabon

Printed in the United States of America
LB
10 9 8 7 6 5 4 3 2 1

Contents

Foreword vii

Preface xi

Introduction xv

1   Cats Are Sluts? 1

2   The Shape-Shifter 8

3   Cat Out of Hell 21

4   Feline Familiars 35

5   The Cat Lady–Crazy, Sexy, Queer 43

6   Cats, Kink, and Kitten Play 63

7   Hex-Ray Vision and the Feline Gaze 80

8   Art Cats–Sex and the Sphinx 88

9   Feline Glamour (Magic) 95

10   Sex Kittens and Painted Cats–Untamed Eroticism 106

11   The Black Cat 113

12   Bloody Kisses–Vampires, Werecats, and Cat People 119

13   Tricksters, Shifters, and Femmes Fatales 129

14   Ailuromancy–Divination with Cats 133

15   Hello Kitty and the Cult of Cute 139

16   Cat's Call 148

17   Pussy Hats and Homocats. 153

18   Tomcats and Feline Casanovas 161

19   Animality and the Mystical Digital. 168

20   Clawing Her Way Out–The Politics of Liberation 173

     Tail's End 179

     Selected Bibliography 190

Foreword

As I sit here swooning over the wise and witty tome you have in your paws, one of my own two feline familiars is lying on top of the couch next to me, left arm a furred Fibonacci curl under her chin, the other extended before her in some sort of horizontal salute of solidarity. Though to the best of my knowledge she cannot read, I think she would very much appreciate *Cat Call's* message: namely, that cats are not only worthy of our care and consideration but that they are slinky keys that can unlock our understanding about the ways in which society has tried to blame, tame, and reclaim so-called "feminine" forces of nature for centuries.

This fluffy companion of mine happens to be named after the surrealist painter Remedios Varo. A famous kitty aficionado herself, Varo infused her work with images of witches, women alchemists, lady explorers, and many, many cats, fascinated as she was by ideas of female magic and personal transformation. So, too, is this author. In the words that Kristen J. Sollée has written—her books, essays, and articles (as well as the tremendous class she teaches at The New School)—she continues to show us how sexuality and symbolism are the ingredients of a spell that can shift our notions of selfhood and enable us to fill a lifetime with many lives (nine, perhaps.)

Kristen and I first bonded over our mutual infatuation with witches and feminism in all of their complexity. Since our first fateful discussion about sex and sorcery in a SoHo teahouse circa 2014, I've watched in awe as she has ceaselessly displayed an irresistible blend of rigorous scholarship and ribald humor in the expression of her ideas—not to mention countless acts of generosity toward myself and other writers, makers, and proud oddballs who are lucky enough to be included in her creative coven.

Mostly, I've been impressed by her unstoppable devotion to shamelessness. No one writes about the subjects of sexuality, desire, shadow, and diabolism with such relish, and when I read her words I feel both smarter and less afraid of my own "taboo" feelings and thoughts. Like a cat, Kristen sees in the dark, and she guides us gracefully forward with her vision of unapologetic feminine power.

It's only fitting then that Kristen's fascinations have gone feline, for these creatures represent so many of the notions she's been batting around over the course of her career. Throughout history, cats have been worshiped and trivialized, adored and abhorred, sexualized and neutered. As *Cat Call* illustrates, these animals are both terrestrial and spiritual, and our treatment of them directly relates to our often conflicting ideas about women and femmes—and the places and spaces they ought to occupy.

I was reminded again of Remedios Varo as I read this book— both the artist and my magical housemate. In a letter to "Father of Wicca" Gerald Gardner, Varo (the human, that is) wrote of her own witchcraft experiments, wherein she combined seemingly disparate elements such as an armchair, a crocodile skull, and a diamond-encrusted pipe into an organized domestic cosmos:

> I have a solar system . . . which I can move at will, knowing beforehand the effects I can generate, though at times the unpredictable is generated, provoked by the rapid

trajectory of an unexpected meteor across my established order. The meteor is none other than my cat, but little by little I have been able to master this haphazard factor . . .

So too has Kristen, with *Cat Call*, constructed her own solar system of eclectic marvels, and so has she somehow managed to master this feral meteor of a muse. These pages of hers will take you on a curious, deliciously circuitous trail filled with all sorts of intriguing spots to stop and curl up in contemplation. You will scamper from Catwoman's lair to Leonor Fini's studio. You will pause for a bit at the temple of Bastet and then rub up against the cult of Hello Kitty. You will strut around your home in leopard print and then prowl through the streets in a pink pussy hat.

This book is intrepid, graceful, and claw-sharp. Let its insights zigzag between your mind and your soul, your loins and your lap, and you will assuredly be left pondering and purring.

Preface

The cat. A sensual shape-shifter. A beloved familiar. A canny hunter, aloof, tail aloft, stalking vermin. A satanic accomplice. A social media darling. A euphemism for reproductive parts. An epithet for the weak. A knitted—and contested—hat on millions of marchers, pink pointed ears poking skyward. Cats and cat references are ubiquitous in art, pop culture, politics, and the occult, and throughout history, they have most often been coded female.

But why?

I found myself newly engaged with this question while researching my last book, *Witches, Sluts, Feminists: Conjuring the Sex Positive*. In nearly every subject and source, cats prowled the margins. They have been revered as magical beings and reviled as evil sorceresses (witches). They have symbolized heightened female sexuality and forbidden eroticism (sluts). They have offered potent imagery for political movements (feminists). Cats could have easily found a forever home in any part of *Witches, Sluts, Feminists*, but they called for their own dedicated volume.

Cat Call: Reclaiming the Feral Feminine is an exploration of the untamed crossroads where "the feline" and "the feminine" mingle and make magic. From ancient Egypt to early modern Venice to Edo Japan, the witch trials to the Women's March, Catwoman to cat ladies, kitten play to cat conventions, *Cat Call* tracks the cat's circuitous connection to women and femininity through a magical lens. By combining historical research, pop culture and art analyses, and original interviews, this book uncovers what the "feral feminine" might mean to witches, sluts, feminists, artists, historians, philosophers, cat ladies, and cat lovers today.

Because the cat is not a linear creature, hers is not a linear tale. This book is not an exercise in teleology, or an attempt to create a single grand narrative. If dominant forms of nonfiction inquiry require structural rigidity, then *Cat Call* is an exercise in curvature, in cycles that ebb and flow, in concentric rings that expand and contract, like the bodies of these most limber creatures—and the circles cast by practitioners of magic to manifest their desires.

I structured this book to be as fluid as the dangerous curves of the feline form. It is as much a joyful strut through history as a cautionary tale. It is as much for people who believe in magic, the supernatural, and the unexplainable as for atheists, skeptics, and those who base their beliefs strictly in science. It is as much about femininity as ultimately about humanity—and animality.

Cat Call is so named not only because this inquiry beckoned me in, but for feline vocalizations and sexist exclamations. In its most common usage, a catcall is an intrusive and objectifying comment most often uttered at women by men on the street. It can involve a wolf whistle or shouted compliment. It can be nasty and jarring, while some might find it amusing or an ego boost. It transforms based upon perspective and person. Like *Witches, Sluts, Feminists, Cat Call* also attempts to recast the aspersions in its title as words with liberating potential.

This book aims to rescue pejorative understandings of the feline and the feminine from myth and history and looks to philosophy, political ideology, and a multiplicity of magical practices for clues on how to do this. It is an inherently political project.

Although cats themselves may be apolitical—apathetic even to our machinations—what cats stir in us is anything but. *Cat Call* seeks to uncover the ways in which the feline-feminine connection might be mined for liberatory practices of the public and private kind.

The catalysts for this book came in many forms: animal, human, etheric. First and foremost, I am deeply grateful to all the feline-loving folks who agreed to share their stories in these pages. To my family and friends (even the cat haters!) who read drafts, sent feline factoids and #catsofinstagram posts at all hours of the night, and/or helped me shape the content of this book: Kathleen, Bill, Charlie, Morgan, Lila, Micol, Sabrina, Tina, Pam, Pieter, and too many more to mention—thank you! I am also grateful to Peter Turner and Weiser Books for believing in my vision of the feral feminine and to my students at The New School for inspiring me to see every inquiry with fresh eyes. Finally, this acknowledgments section would not be complete without a love note to my cat: Cherie, you have brought so much veracity to this project and joy to my life. I'll start getting up at 6 a.m. to play with you once this book is out, I swear.

Introduction

Hearth keepers, demonic harbingers, otherworldly emissaries—cats and women have been culturally inscribed with the same attributes for millennia. This enduring kinship between the feline and the feminine shows up in our mythologies that give goddesses feline faces and cat attendants. It's central to our stereotypes of the cat lady, the cougar, and the sex kitten, which populate a stifling spectrum between scorned singlehood and revered sex appeal. It's infused into our language: *catty, pussy, kittenish* are words deployed to pin down feminine behavior and female bodies through playful, provocative, and pejorative feline allegories. It's in the ineffable magic and mesmeric power we attribute to both cats and women.

Circled like a serpent—a purring ouroboros—or arched into an S curve, the sacred geometry of the cat is as worship-worthy today as it was a thousand years ago. Run your fingers along the sleek perimeter of any feline who will have you and dare not be impressed by their flexibility, self-starting motor, iridescent irises; the way they can compress their ribs and contract their shoulders to shift in shape and fit into impossible places, then expand out again, fur puffed up in a protective halo; the cries they create meant to mimic human babies and mesmerize and master adults in the process. Some shy away from such encounters due to allergies, superstition, or straight-up malice, but those who belong to the ever-growing cult of the cat know what it is to be bewitched.

Few animals have slunk into the annals of myth and history like the cat. They seem to serve no practical purpose compared to other four-legged friends. We don't really eat them or wear them and can't force them into our service. By all accounts, they have instead forced us into theirs. The ties that bind humans to cats are more tenuous. Something else is afoot. Because ever since the first wildcat, *Felis silvestris lybica*, encroached on human encampments in the Fertile Crescent 10,000 years ago, we've been elevating them to idol status—and relegating them to the depths of Hell. Cats began as scavengers on the edge of town and ended up clawing their way into our hearths and hearts.

Today, not much has changed. *Felis silvestris lybica* evolved into *Felis catus*, the domestic house cat, but they're still after our leftovers, and many of us are still starved for their love. Well over 50 million people own cats in the United States alone, and estimates place the number of cats around the world at six hundred million and counting. Such overwhelming statistics speak to the universality of the cat-human relationship, and yet, across Europe, Asia, and North America, women have long been ascribed *cattributes*, and cats have been spoken of in feminine tones.

Even before I stroked the coat of a single plush playmate, I sensed a deep connection to these cryptic creatures. As a child, I would whisper clumsy incantations into fuzzy ears. I'd immerse myself in feline lore from far-off places. I'd sing *Cats* at the top of my lungs. Later, I discovered sex and power through a certain whip-wielding alter ego. And I learned how much I desired unbridled freedom in the same way my meowing loves would squirm out of my arms to dart into darkened corners, uninterested in pleasing me.

My affinity for cats was not only about the animals themselves but also what they represented. Cats have been my companions, but cats have also been ciphers that helped me unravel the complexities of womanhood warped by a sexist world. They helped me conjure the kind of femininity that felt at home in my skin. At the heart of this alchemical relationship between the feline and the feminine is a wildness, a refusal of patriarchal prescriptions, which has been ambivalently embraced and suppressed since the cat first entered our cultural consciousness centuries ago.

This is the breeding ground for the feral feminine.

At first glance, the feral feminine is a femininity that refuses domestication. See it in incisors that aren't ground down, a larynx that unleashes too loudly, a sexual appetite that refuses to heel. To be feral is to be untamed, and to be feminine is to contain multitudes—which can, but doesn't have to, involve various modes of creation, adornment, caretaking, and intuition.

You'll find the feral feminine in places where the feline and the feminine are alternately pampered and adored, hunted and subjugated, downplayed and totally ignored—often at the same time. Pin down just one of these manifestations, and it has already become something else entirely.

Although the feral feminine originated with the association between women and domestic cats, it is equally embodied by any feline (lions, tigers, lynxes, leopards, cheetahs . . .) and any person who might partake in feminine expression (cis and trans women and men, nonbinary femmes . . .). It may be many things, but it is not bound to one kind of body.

Reclaiming the feral feminine begins with diving deep into myth and history while being wary of the distortions of misogyny. It requires sinking your teeth into the colorful lies that have been spun about untamed women, feminine folks, and their feline brethren. Revel in them; subvert them. It is to reframe accusations of animality not as sexism, but as a gift, for animals do not fear death, they do not start wars, they aren't hell-bent on destroying the earth. Such an act of reclaiming requires channeling primal instincts to fuel this overcoming.

If you're new to this subject, much of what we'll uncover has merely been hiding in plain sight. It's in ancestral myths. It's in paintings that hang in the Metropolitan Museum of Art. It's in the classics of literature, popular films, fashion, and music videos. It's in the very language we use to describe femininity—as evidenced by many a celebrity feature. Famous actresses, as they're often portrayed, are apparently some of the most feline folks on the planet. Angela Bassett, for example, has "huge feline eyes." Charlize Theron has "cat-like cheekbones." Laverne Cox's stiletto nails are "claws" that are "feline and powerful."

Catlike language has long been employed to conjure feminine sex appeal, but it's not only erotics that drive our feline comparisons. Sometimes cats are in the work of a female creatrix whose medium is language. Joan Didion has "fantastically long, feline sentences"; Jane Austen has an "indefinite feline suggestion" to her work; and even Seshat, the Egyptian goddess credited with inventing writing, envelops herself in a leopard or cheetah skin as she scrivens.

What is it about feminine creation that is catlike? It likely links back to the fecundity and maternal marvels of female cats. They never kill their darlings but risk hide and hair for them so that they might flourish beyond their humble beginnings. It's an apt metaphor, really, for all those looking to get their work out of their heads and onto the page without too much bloodshed or self-recrimination.

When you start speaking in "cat," you enter a realm of punning and double entendres, where language stalks and plays as you bat it around in your brain. It can be overly cute, or it can slice to the heart of the matter and kill. Cats move and meander in mysterious ways. What writer wouldn't hope that every sentence they wrote would slink and spiral and convey a kind of majesty that wasn't overstated but always enthralling? My fever dream is that cat essence conveys in this curious little book. It is above all a love letter to these languid creatures and all that they represent.

We'll start this search for the feral feminine in the ancient world by way of the twenty-first century, because history, like the cat, moves in circles and cycles.

Cats Are Sluts?

#catsaresluts trying to seduce you

#catsaresluts because they can rub up against anyone's ankles

#catsaresluts they don't care who they go home with

#catsaresluts and dogs are faithful

D ozens of proclamations on Twitter refer to the licentious nature of cats. Tweet after tweet chastises cats for licking themselves or sitting with their legs splayed, private parts peeking out through downy fluff. Some tweets opine how a cat can have kittens at such a young age. Some tweets complain that a cat can play nice for a nuzzle one moment, then stalk away haughtily the next. Other tweets affirm the indecency of a cat's distaste for monogamy.

When the #catsaresluts hashtag first began to trend in late March of 2013, there was a common thread to the majority of posts: an outrage—or faux outrage, at least—about a cat's lack of shame.

For some reason, cat nature aligns in our minds with a predilection for pleasure. To be catlike is to be contemptuous of sexual mores. It is to be unbowed by propriety and repressive body politics.

It is to be wild and unrestrained, in a constant state of arousal. There are no scientific studies that suggest cats are any more or less amorous than other animals, but the idea of cats as hypersexual beasts persists.

My cat is not even 1 and she's pregnant #catsaresluts

My cat shags 3 tom cats a night #catsaresluts

Curiosity killed your virginity #catsaresluts

Female cats have long been perceived as paragons of fertility. They are induced ovulators, so mating can trigger conception during any one of their many heat cycles throughout the year. They can reach sexual maturity as early as four months, and if left to their own devices, can have an average of twelve kittens per year that spring from the seed of multiple males. Add to that a cat's audible courtship and arousal rituals, and it's not hard to understand why cats—and female cats in particular—have been slapped with the *slut* label.

Slut, however, has become a shape-shifting epithet. It can be a hateful label, used to police and punish women for their perceived or actual sexual expression (slut-shaming). It can be a feminist rallying cry, used to highlight issues of bodily autonomy and sex positivity (SlutWalk). It can be a tongue-in-cheek sobriquet (Love you, slut!). Although it can be used to describe almost anyone, it is mostly a gendered term to laud or lash out at women who seem to indulge in sexual behavior that has historically been decried as improper, dangerous even, and worthy of punishment.

When taken at face value, the #catsaresluts trend is merely an outlet for lighthearted humor. Scratch below the surface, however, and there's much more at stake. Many of the tweets subtly reinforce biases against female sexuality by referring to all cats as if they were female. Feline behavior, then, is seen as repellent because of its proximity to femininity. In effect, #catsaresluts puts a cute face on sexist stereotyping and encourages its dissemination.

Twitter users are by no means the first to disparage cats and women, though. The same kind of misogynistic malice was actually directed toward female felines over a thousand years ago by the father of Western philosophy himself.

As far as we know, cats have been sluts since at least the fourth century BC. When Aristotle documented the particulars of the animal kingdom in *History of Animals*, he made sure to let on that he viewed female cats as less virtuous than other mammals. In exacting detail, the Greek philosopher explored all manner of animal behaviors, even offering ample word count dedicated to the ins and outs of stag, seal, and snake mating habits. There is little added judgment on his part when describing most copulation behaviors, save for his discussion of cats.

"Cats do not copulate with a rearward presentment on the part of the female, but the male stands erect and the female puts herself underneath him," Aristotle writes. In a prurient aside he interjects, "and, by the way, the female cat is peculiarly lecherous, and wheedles the male on to sexual commerce, and caterwauls during the operation."

Straightforward as it may seem, Aristotle's jeer isn't just about cats. His *History of Animals* is significant not only because it is a foundational exploration of the animal kingdom, but because it is "simultaneously an exposition of what it means to be human," explains classics scholar Edith Hall in *Aristotle's Way: How Ancient Wisdom Can Change Your Life*. Aristotle was a firm believer in the inferiority of women, so his commentary has implications that stretch beyond the bounds of species. Whatever the Greek philosopher had seen to inspire his prejudicial view of cats—probably just actual cats having sex—coupled with his views of women solidified the distasteful link between frisky felines and human females. Following his colorful comment, the two would be cast as beleaguered bedfellows for years to come, suspect for innate desires they could not—or would not—curb.

"Aristotle's association of cats with heightened and unseemly sexuality among women became absorbed into the common wisdom," author of *Perilous Chastity: Women and Illness in Pre-Enlightenment Art and Medicine* Laurinda S. Dixon writes.

In addition to affirming Aristotle's role in shaping how we connect cats, sex, and women, Dixon also suggests that the cat can be read as a "symbol for the uterus." She reveals how Western culture came to view the uterus as "a roving, amoral creature," drawing from Plato's description of hysteria in women and the wayward uterus as "the animal within them."

Even before the time of Aristotle, "wandering womb disease," also known as hysteria, was the catchall cause of many ailments found in women. The belief was that if one's uterus wasn't anchored down by childbearing or chastity, it could be unleashed within the body, laying waste to the physical and emotional health of its owner. Hysteria could be the cause of anxiety, panic attacks, depression, and mood swings. Hysteria could also be the cause of an overactive libido. There was no end to the ways this sexist diagnosis supposedly impacted a woman's health.

In *Evil Sisters: The Threat of Female Sexuality and the Cult of Manhood*, author Bram Dijkstra cites the writings of 19th-century medical professor Augustus Gardner on hysteria, which suggest that "personal pollution" was just as much the cause for waking the inner wildcat within women as not fulfilling their motherly duties. Every precaution was taken to keep "that veritable black panther of feminine sexual evil" from overtaking the female of the species, Dijkstra explains, which meant keeping a close watch on all women's sexual activity.

Cats, then, have not only been symbols for sexual women, but for an organ often associated with women's sexual worth and sexual evil. Yes, women can be cats, but many women also have a cat within them, living inside their most sensitive of regions, just lying in wait. Whether said cat decides to procreate or pounce is entirely up to chance.

Aristotle's snide remark about cats isn't the sole reason we continue to associate felines with female carnality. The philosopher's prejudicial sentiments no doubt infected the minds of men throughout the Western world, but they would be compounded by early Christians denouncing all that pagan cultures held dear, particularly goddesses of fertility who consorted with cats.

The link between cats, sex, and the divine feminine is as old as recorded history itself. Felines of all stripes were believed to be paragons of procreation, so they made excellent allies for fecund deities. Early visions of the feral feminine survive today in the form of cave paintings, carved statues, amulets, architecture, and funeral relics.

A sculpture from Neolithic Turkey, known as the Seated Woman of Çatalhöyük, shows a voluptuous mother, breasts heavy, belly round, face kind—a sister of the Venus of Willendorf perhaps?—each hand resting on the head of a leopard.

The Ishtar Gate of ancient Babylon venerating the goddess of love, sex, fertility, and war features 120 of the lions associated with Ishtar prowling across the processional bricks leading up to the arch.

In Hindu temples from the early first millennium, reliefs show the violent yet nurturing mother goddess Durga riding a tiger or lion.

Wood carvings from the Viking age depict Freya, Norse goddess of fertility, flanked by two cat attendants who pull her on a throne, and surviving statuettes of Roman mother goddess Cybele portray her in a chariot led by lions.

The felines that accompany these otherworldly women signal how both parties were perceived: mighty, magical, sensual. Such connections were taken to greater heights in ancient Egypt, when sacred women weren't merely accompanied by cats, but became them.

Egyptian mythology bestows a multitude of deities with feline features. The mother goddess Isis is occasionally depicted as a cat, as are Mut, Hathor, Wadjet, Pakhet, and Tefnut. Gender matters in these cases, as "feline deities are predominately female," asserts Aleid De Jong in *The Oxford Essential Guide to Egyptian Mythology*—although there are a few male deities who have feline characteristics as well.

As early as the Second Dynasty, Bast, the lioness goddess of war, held court in the hearts and minds of the people in Lower Egypt. In Upper Egypt, the lioness Sekhmet filled a similar pugilistic role. When the two territories finally united, these goddesses began to diverge.

Sekhmet, protectress of the pharaohs, kept her lion head and a glowing solar disk on her headpiece topped with a uraeus cobra. Bast, later known as Bastet, morphed into a cat-headed goddess, revered as a fierce protectress, symbolizing motherhood and fertility.

Some historians speculate that Bast was initially a lioness and her features softened to become a cat because lions migrated away from the Nile delta and domesticated cats become more and more popular as pets. Others wager it might have something to do with differentiating her from Sekhmet. Egyptologist Ruth Schumann Antelme has a different take altogether.

In *Sacred Sexuality in Ancient Egypt: The Erotic Secrets of the Forbidden Papyrus* the author proposes that "divine lioness"

Tefnut-Sekhmet, "an independent, untamed, and zealous deity," was defanged and transformed into a cat. Desiring to sow her wild oats, she left her father Ra to "romp as she pleased" in the desert. After some time passed (and litters of cubs had been produced from her wanderings), both Ra and the people of Egypt began to miss the presence of the goddess. To remedy her absence, her brothers Shu and Thoth forcibly brought her back to civilization, on the way plunging her into sacred waters that would eventually quell some of her wildness. Back on dry land, the goddess formerly known as Tefnut-Sekhmet "emerged tamed and in the form of a ravishing young woman—or a charming and cuddly cat," now named Bastet.

Still overflowing with fecundity, Bastet's sexuality became less about her own needs and more a wellspring for human couples to draw their procreative forces from. Under the watchful eye of Ra, she became less ferocious, less sexually explorative, but not entirely benign. Antelme describes Bastet as the "tamed but still uncontrollable" cat form of Sekhmet. The two feline goddesses are two sides of the same coin: the maternal cat and the voluptuous lion. "Kindly is she as Bast, terrible is she as Sekhmet," recites M. Oldfield Howey in *The Cat in Magic, Mythology, and Religion*, drawing from an ancient Philae text.

In either form, these feline deities represent sexual expression at its most freewheeling and at its most productive, and they were worshipped without judgment. Bast and Sekhmet would undergo a variety of changes throughout their tenure in ancient Egypt, but by the time of the ancient Greeks and Aristotle, the female feline began to take on an entirely different hue.

Our perception of the feral feminine—like the feral feminine itself—is always shifting shape.

The Shape-Shifter

Seven cervical.

Thirteen thoracic.

Seven lumbar.

Three sacral.

Twenty-one caudal.

Vertebrae stacked.

Strung together, sinew packed, the fearful symmetry of a cat by nature shifts shape. Clavicles float free, anchored only in muscle. Ribs tighten then protract. Low and flat, lean and narrow, coiled serpentine, hair-on-end exalting in taking-up-space—that is the cat. These compressible creatures are shape-shifters, their physicality fluid, befitting any situation or inquisitive whim. Whiskers splayed wide, a cat senses when exactly a transformation should begin.

Hunters by design, felines are built to track prey into the smallest of spaces and inflate their silhouettes at will. Cats may now make our homes their nocturnal paradise, leaping at laser pointers,

spiraling into boxes, and attacking passing feet like mortal enemies, but little has changed since they've lived among us. See a
tawny figure slipping by, undetected, between cracks in the stone
sanctuary at Delphi to sit at the feet of the sibyl herself. Or sense
the outline of a single gray tail flicking from beneath the wood
foundation of a Japanese longhouse or an inflated black specter
amid the grain stores of an English cellar, besting an invisible foe.
Cats move between territories, between worlds, becoming what
they need to be in the moment.

Building upon this innate ability to change form, folklore around
the world has frequently attached a shape-shifting power to cats.
When these felines are feminine, this mercurial effect is amplified.

In ancient Greek mythology, the sphinx had dangerous allure.
With the body of a lion, avian wings, and a woman's head, she
was the keeper of knowledge who could see into men's souls. For
years she crafted riddles at the gates of Thebes. Her wily wordplay
would be the death of thousands of men, until Oedipus cracked her
code and she crashed her body on the rocks in resignation.

In Edo Japan, the *bakeneko yujo* were shape-shifting cat courtesans. Rumor had it that in the pleasure districts of Tokyo, customers would awaken in the middle of the night to find the woman
with whom they had paid to share a bed hunched before a shoji
screen, vertical slits lit by moonlight, tearing open a fish carcass.
Sometimes, male clients would even be swallowed whole by these
ravenous cat women.

Tales of shape-shifting cats were numerous during the early
modern European witch hunts, too, when witches were thought to
send out their feline forms to inflict harm. You could never be sure
if the cat who found its way to your door was a bashful associate
after TLC or a demonic woman on a mission of nefarious recon.
(Best to feed her either way.)

Presenting across cultures, shape-shifters break free from the confines of a single fixed physicality. Those who morph their forms defy the stifling binaries that organize the known world and reveal how tenuous all boundaries are.

But what defines a shape-shifter, apart from literally shifting shape?

According to Brent A. Stypczynski in *The Modern Literary Werewolf: A Critical Study of the Mutable Motif*, a shape-shifter is "a figure, whether human or otherwise, that is capable of altering its physical appearance without the aid of make-up, surgery, or prosthetics, often crossing species, gender and racial boundaries."

To Serinity Young, shape-shifters carry a specific gendered dimension. "Terrifying in their physical fluidity, shape-shifters are perversions of nature, belonging to the category of the monstrous-feminine," she explains in *Women Who Fly: Goddesses, Witches, Mystics, and Other Airborne Females*. These include "women with both animal and human features . . . sphinxes of Greco-Roman mythology, [and] demonesses of all times."

The feminine, feline shape-shifters introduced above all share a penchant for mischief. Their ability to play with words, with sexuality, with physiology allows them to entrance, ensnare, and even overcome aspects of patriarchal rule—although these hybrid beings often met their ends at the hands of men.

"Shape-shifting breaches fundamental boundaries," Young elaborates. "They are indifferent to differentiation, violating the established order, including the order of gender." So what is it about femininity—or perceptions of femininity at least—that aligns with shape-shifting and perpetual motion?

The feline and the feminine are famously forced to stretch and shrink, flatten and swell to survive in the landscapes they inhabit. Embodying either category requires the ability to move between worlds. Liminal living, *feliminality*, means slipping in and out of sight, between legs, and into spaces where they can never quite follow you. It means navigating how not to be at the beck and call of the master, even as some days you may sit and purr at his feet, ready to engage your claws.

All this requires a great measure of flexibility, and yet there are limits. Myth, magic, and popular culture tell us that there are at least six rules of engagement for the shape-shifters that haunt our dreams and screens. Keep these in mind as we continue our descent into the feral feminine.

1. Be Careful What You Witch For

Shape-shifting isn't always a two-way street.

In Celtic lore, the Cat Sìth was a mystical black cat with a white spot on its chest thought by some to be a shape-shifting witch who could suck out the souls from dead bodies. This witch could turn from a cat back to a human only eight times. The ninth? She would be stuck on all fours.

2. Pain Can Be Permanent

An injury to a shape-shifter can remain despite subsequent transformations.

In the early modern witch-hunting text, the *Malleus Malefi-carum*, author Heinrich Kramer spins a tale of a woodcutter in Strasburg who is attacked by three vicious cats. In a panic, the woodcutter uses the fore and aft of his axe to fight off the cats: hitting one on the legs, one on the head, and one on the back. Not long after, two magistrates approach and arrest the man for causing grievous injury to three women of the town, who expressed injuries on their back, legs, and head. Local law was quite familiar with the shape-shifting abilities of witches, so once the man confessed to his fight with the demonic cats, he was set free. The women were left to lick their wounds.

3. Become a Wildcat in the Sack (Literally)

Arousal can incite a transformation, so shape-shifters must beware the bedroom.

Carnal heat causes some female shape-shifters to boil over. As Stypczynski notes, the shape-shifter archetype "has transgressive erotic undertones, especially when it appears in werewolf stories and sixteenth-century witchcraft trials—with witches turning into cats to enter their victims' bedrooms." The women in the films *Cat People* (released in 1942 and remade in 1982) were driven to eat their lovers alive if they gave in to their sexual stirrings. To prevent such carnage, these werecats in women form had to discipline themselves with strict abstinence.

4. Flesh Can Be Refashioned

Shape-shifting can occur through both a literal and figurative refashioning of flesh.

We often think of shape-shifters changing physical form, but despite traditional definitions, transformations can be sparked by a simple costume change. Clothing can completely reframe the way we are perceived by the world (and by ourselves) so enacting a glamour spell can imbue humans with feline force and the aesthetic elegance of cats.

5. Transform to Transcend Trauma

Shape-shifting can serve as a way to cope with traumatic or trying circumstances, and in the process even empower others.

Many shape-shifters in fiction and folklore transform for survival. The comic series *Cihualyaomiquiz, The Jaguar,* by Mexican-American illustrator Laura Molina, depicts the Mesoamerican shape-shifter known as the *nahual.* Through a ritualistic transformation, Linda Rivera, a lawyer by day, becomes The Jaguar by night, a superheroine who embodies the spirit of "Chicana Feminist Anarchy." Rivera shifts shape so she can fight neo-Nazis and the California government from attacking the human rights of immigrants and people of color. By tapping into her indigenous, shape-shifting heritage, she attempts to liberate her community.

6. Genderflux over Gender Fixity

When the borders between animal and human are in flux, so are the borders between masculine and feminine.

Shape-shifters are by definition gender nonbinary. They have no need to ally with a single gender and are arguably most radical when they eschew gender fixity altogether. However, many feline shape-shifters have historically been female and themselves blur the lines between masculine and feminine through action and/or dress. Of all attributes of the shape-shifter, these gender shifts inspire the most fear and fascination within societies with rigid sex roles.

Life's a bitch, now so am I.
–Catwoman, *Batman Returns*

I was a nine-year-old girl wielding a whip after dark in a subur-
ban cul-de-sac. Compelled by Catwoman to molt my child skin, I
leapt with clumsy bravado into new flesh. First, there was a shiny
black unitard fit with imitation stitches applied with pearlized
puffy paint. Second came a pair of kitten-heeled boots, suede and
slouched. Third, a pointy-eared, rubber mask stretched over the
crown of my head to be tightened around my throat with Velcro
strips. It wasn't an exact replica, but it was enough. I slipped outside, and the night enveloped me like a wave.

Batman Returns was darkening theaters the summer of 1992,
and my commitment to Gotham City's gothic camp was so great I
swiped the promotional cardboard cutout for the film, languished
in line to behold the Batmobile at the local mall, and sought out
every *Fangoria* issue with a mere mention of Catwoman on the
cover. I filled spiral notebooks with collages of movie stills and
transcriptions of Michelle Pfeiffer's purred bon mots. My room? A
lair. My new tuxedo kitten? Bruce Wayne.

The ritual of getting into character alone was grounding.
Although I didn't feel like a woman by any means, dressing up like
Catwoman brought me one step closer to feeling like a cat—a far
more desirable identity. While my single mother slept in the room
across the hall, I transformed as my Angora-Himalayan looked on,
eyes alive in the night. Stalking the borders of animal and human,
hero and villain, fantasy and reality, I felt safer in my new costume
than I did in child clothes, divested from my fallible form.

No doubt Selina Kyle did, too.

First introduced in DC Comics' *Batman* #1 published in 1940,
Catwoman was initially a babely, raven-haired jewel thief known
as The Cat. By issue #2 she was called Cat-Woman, and by issue

#3 she had donned a furry, purple cat's head and cape to carry out her crimes. It wasn't until 1947 that she got a stylized mask. The catsuit came later.

There are divergent backstories that explain why Selina Kyle became Catwoman in the first place, but they each involve an overcoming. For Kyle, becoming catlike was pure survival. Whether she was acting out after a case of amnesia, breaking away from an abusive husband or vicious pimp, or escaping a childhood of poverty and incarceration, transforming her vulnerable human body allowed her to gain control and reinforce her resolve with a second skin—to lick her wounds, to enact payback.

Catwoman would set her sights on female foes, but men remained her most frequent targets. In the Detective Comics issue "Black Cat Crimes" from 1947, Catwoman tries to blackmail three Gotham City magnates: a furrier, a circus owner, and a shipping tycoon. When she fails to get their money, she wreaks havoc on their businesses, gleefully incinerating merchandise and terrorizing customers and crew members. In a poignant denouement, she escapes from the top of the Statue of Liberty, repurposing this feminine symbol of freedom for her own transgressive ends.

Years later in "The Catwoman's Black Magic," published in 1966, Selina Kyle gets another woman—this time, eternal good girl and Superman fan Lois Lane—to turn against the man she loves. But it isn't until the late 1960s, at the height of the women's liberation movement, that Catwoman finally voices her vigilantism in gendered terms.

"We all have a common cause—a common enemy," she hisses in a 1969 comic to the Feline Furies, a pack of female convicts. "Men! It was men who led us astray—men who put us behind bars like caged tigers! Now I give you a chance to strike back—with bared fangs and clawed paws!" (The issue also features

Catwoman announcing that Batman has "lost the battle of the sexes" on the cover.)

Although Selina Kyle's anger against the sexist system is not deemed worthy of attention, Catwoman's rage, voiced in terms of feline ferocity, is formidable. Her teeth sharpen to become fangs, her fingernails curl into claws. If Kyle was voiceless before, her roar is deafening now.

In Tim Burton's film *Batman Returns*, Catwoman's character is still out for blood. Introduced as a meek, disheveled secretary, Kyle is overworked, underpaid, and ignored by the corporate suits she works for at Schreck Industries. In an attempt to get ahead by burning the midnight oil, Kyle's curiosity over a few protected files gets her killed when she is violently pushed out a window by her power-mad boss Max Schreck. Left for dead on the alley floor, she is subsequently brought back to life by a gang of otherworldly cats and undergoes a transformation back at her apartment.

Smashing porcelain collectibles, eviscerating stuffed animals, and spray-painting her pink walls black, Kyle systematically annihilates objects that symbolize passivity, fragility, and femininity. Destroying her domicile, the archetypal seat of femininity, Kyle—now Catwoman—must build a new home that reflects a rejection of her former vulnerable self. The answering machine that plays an ad about pleasing a man through perfume, the delicate dollhouse, the pastel kitten T-shirt in her closet—they've all got to go.

To become catlike, Kyle must shed the aspects of womanhood that do not serve her. She rails against the trappings of femininity that were preyed upon by men and corporate capitalism, the things she feels left her open to abuse.

Once Kyle is finished crafting her new costume out of a patent leather rain slicker and fashioning her claws out of sewing needles,

Catwoman stands triumphant in the window of her apartment, the transformation complete. She has quite literally replaced her soft pink underbelly with a thick black coat. Her body shines like an oil slick. She stretches into an X, lit up by the remaining fuchsia letters of a neon sign she has only partially destroyed. It now aptly reads: "hell here."

In eighteenth-century Venice, a radically different kind of cat costume offered a similar opportunity for transformation, transgression, and violent play.

Once a year, between the Christian holidays of Saint Stephen's Day and Ash Wednesday, the people of Venice and visitors from around the world would join in revelry and social inversion, donning masks to become whoever—and whatever—they pleased. At Carnival, men could be women, women could be men, the rich could slum it, and the poor could take on the adornments of wealth. One such character that was spotted carousing in cafés around the Piazza San Marco was the *gnaga*.

Named after the Venetian word for the sound of a cat's meow—*gnau*—the *gnaghe* were men who dressed as women in voluminous skirts and beads, shouted obscenities in feline timbres, and were even said to carry baskets of kittens with them to heighten their femme appeal. These "men in dresses who preened and fought like cats in heat" remain something of a mystery, however, notes James H. Johnson in *Venice Incognito: Masks in the Serene Republic*. Were they out to "mock their social or sexual opposites" asks Johnson, or did the *gnaghe* wear "an honest disguise, a mask that told the truth according to their desires and in defiance of social norms?"

At the time, Venetian class hierarchies were rigid, and laws against homosexuality were equally so. Fusing feline iconography and femininity with brute force, the *gnaghe* represented a unique gender expression that was performative and unsettling. They sang popular songs and put on theatrical scenes in the streets, fought one another in public, and were so boisterous and beguiling that passersby would line up to purchase tickets to see them unleash inside cafés.

There are accounts of *gnaghe* painting the town pink throughout the eighteenth century, but these "kitten-carrying drag queens" (as *Culture Trip* calls them) appeared with enough frequency to frighten officials in the 1780s. Spies for the government caught wind of more than one *gnaga* engaging in sodomy, and there were other accounts of *gnaghe* being hunted down and beaten within an inch of their lives.

Viewed by some as curiosities and by others as beasts, the *gnaghe* confounded laypeople and authorities alike. Did mimicking the cries of a cat and squeezing into petticoats offer men license to fraternize more freely with other men? Or was it just another example of Carnival's outré trappings that failed to truly challenge social taboos?

Amid the pungent, winding canals, these hellions flaunted their illicit sexual affairs, their hot tempers, their genderqueer attire—and they used cat symbology to telegraph their femininity to a world that was ready to accept them as entertainment, but not equals.

Today, Venice remains a city that wears its feline history on its sleeve. The official flag of the region features a winged lion—as it has for centuries. Tourist outposts and artisan shops alike offer ornate cat carnival masks. Postcards and paintings boast images of feline *Medico della Peste* (plague doctors), kitten *streghetta* (little witches), and courtly ladies drawn as cats dolled up in cake-like tiered fashions of bygone eras.

Living cats still populate the canals of the maritime republic, too. Ships from the Middle East likely introduced the species to Venice's bustling port, and by the fourteenth century, they found notoriety when they were thought by locals to have eradicated the rats that spread the bubonic plague. Cats also found fame from local owners, like Doge Francesco Morosini. Decked in scarlet on the deck of the ship he commanded, Morosini was never without his beloved pussy, Nini, during his tenure between 1688 and 1694. (Incidentally, he never married, and Nini was embalmed with a mouse between her paws after his death. You can visit the tabby's remains at the Museo di Storia Naturale, situated on the Grand Canal.)

Hundreds of years later in the 1960s, British expat Helena Sanders moved to Venice and began advocating for over 38,000 stray cats that lived on the streets. She offered sterilization and medical attention, despite the pushback from local authorities who didn't think there was a cat problem at all. Sanders is credited with being one of the first to practice TNR (Trap, Neuter, Return) in Italy and sparked a feline exodus from the lagoon city.

The remaining feral cats that roam Venetian backstreets symbolize a kind of wildness and autonomy that Venetians have all but lost today in a town dominated by tourism. These cats perch precariously on windows above passing gondoliers, nab discarded morsels of food off dinner tables, mew plaintively at shopkeepers, and slink like spirits without a sound across cobblestones. Each year, the Carnival that begins in February conjures up the days when countless cats skirted the edges of the canals and the *gnaghe*'s heeled boots skittered across the streets.

These human-feline hybrids slashed apart conceptions of gender, sexuality, and species, and offer us a window into shape-shifting through costumery in the eighteenth century.

Like Catwoman, the *gnaghe* used *cattributes* to heighten their femininity—although the results were radically different. For both parties, however, becoming catlike was an avenue to a new life— and liberation—enacted by either escaping the trauma and violence that living in a feminine body had courted or embracing violence in a new feminine form.

Cats electrified Catwoman with the feral impulse to be bold and transgressive, and cats released the *gnaghe*'s riotous, gender-bending behavior. By masking themselves, Catwoman and the *gnaghe* were finally able to unmask, and become who they needed to be.

Cat Out of Hell

The cat is the beautiful devil.

–Charles Bukowski

The Devil teaches women what they are–
or they would teach it to the Devil if he did not know.

–Jules Barbey d'Aurevilly

Hellcats. She-devils. Women and cats straddle the worlds of men and beasts. They are lusty shape-shifters, fickle with affection, who master a host of bodily processes beyond comprehension. Prevailing prejudice has cast women and cats as the Devil's darlings, and as the Devil himself.

Long before medieval treatises depicted cats as evil, and long after the ancient Egyptians worshipped at the altar of a benevolent goddess in feline form, the first woman in Christian mythology was corrupted not by a cat, but by a slit-eyed, hissing confederate in Satan's plan. Shameless, naked, and feral in the Garden of Eden, you could say Eve had a certain feline quality about her. She followed her own instincts. She did not do as she was told. As God and Adam soon found out, she was not as obedient as they would have liked. Eve's curiosity killed the dream of paradise for mankind.

Beliefs about women and cats have followed a serpentine path. Although biologically distinct in numerous ways, cats and snakes share a vertical pupil, a penchant for curling up in a crescent or coil, and are despised in Christianity and deified in the pantheon of pagan religions.

"The Cat and the Serpent are merely two forms of the same allegory," proposes M. Oldfield Howey. He cites a tale from Norse mythology, where Thor is tasked with lifting a colossal cat to prove his strength, which turns out to be a disguised World Serpent, the sea snake so long it encircles the earth. Similarly, the sun god Ra takes the form of a giant cat to kill the snake Apep, who symbolizes darkness and chaos and is known as the World Encircler. "Night is born of day, day of night, light of darkness, darkness of light . . . life of death and death of life," Howey continues. "The cat in repose forms a circle, even as the serpent's head finds and bites its tail again."

These two animals share a parallel history. To the Christian patriarchs, this history was reason enough that the feline of the species would be forced to join the cadre of *animals always up to no good*. (Women were already in said cadre from their humble beginnings as a broken rib.)

The pairing of serpent and feline, femininity and devilry, is all over art of the medieval era. In depicting the Adam and Eve origin story, cats appear opposite snakes in multiple renderings: Hendrick Goltzius's *The Fall of Man*, Wenzel Peter's *Adam and Eve in the Garden of Eden*, and Albrecht Dürer's *Adam and Eve*.

Dürer's engraving from 1504 features Eve fingering an apple passed from a snake coiled around a branch. A cat sits at her feet, its tail curving around her Achilles tendon, mirroring the symmetry of the serpent above. If the snake is metaphorically offering her entrée into the dark side, the cat is quite literally roping her in. Eve is fixated on the apple in the serpent's mouth: enrapt. The cat crouches comfortably beneath her, eyes closed: content. Adam looks worried. God is not pleased.

Cats soon became stand-ins for satanic forces. There need not be a literal serpent in the room to foreshadow unrest: a wide-eyed, unblinking visage and a pair of pointy ears will do. European audiences would soon come to recognize the cat as part of the sisterhood of sinister animals. Artists could skip over the snakes altogether if they pleased.

Domenico Ghirlandaio's fresco of the Last Supper from 1480, for example, shows the cat as a paragon of perfidy. Judas sits across a long banquet table from Jesus and eleven other Apostles. He has yet to be uncovered as a traitor, but a small furry body sits calmly, ominously, behind him, tipping off the audience that all is not well. The cat isn't out of the bag—yet.

Hieronymous Bosch also includes a frightening feline in his vast triptych *The Temptation of St. Anthony* from 1501. Near the woman taunting Anthony with her obscene nudity, a pointy-eared gray cat (Satan?), mouth open in a cry, fangs out, seizes a large fish (Christianity?) in its claws. Whether the cat is satanic or merely a ravenous hunter is up for debate. The scene isn't the focus of the piece, but a telling detail.

By the Middle Ages, the sinful trifecta of witches, cats, and Satan began to materialize.

"The Devil's delicate fondling, the lesser Witch, begotten of the Black Mass after the greater one's disappearance, came and bloomed in all her malignant cat-like grace," rhapsodizes Jules Michelet in *La Sorcière*, a sympathetic recounting of the witch hunts. "This woman is quite the reverse of the other: refined and sidelong in manner, sly and purring demurely, quick also at setting up her back . . . she is naturally base; lewd from her cradle and full of evil daintiness. Her whole life is the expression of those unclean thoughts," Michelet continues.

Those unclean thoughts she had in mind? They might look like your average Friday night. According to the Christian clergy, witches spent most of their time at sabbaths with their sisters in the woods, where they mounted phallic objects, concocted magic unguents, conferred with feline familiars, and maybe even snuck an anal kiss in a dalliance with the Devil (more on that later).

One account that foreshadowed such witchy imaginings is an X-rated tale not fit for the familial pulpit. *Vox in Rama*, a c. 1233 papal decree from Gregory IX, warned the masses about obscene rituals that were allegedly taking place in northern Germany. It regaled readers with details of the carnal meeting between a satanic cat with whom witches would join in apostasy-driven orgies. "This heresy is discordant to all reason, contrary to all piety, odious to all hearts, inimical to all that is in heaven and earth," the text reads, and yet, the people just *had* to know what was going down so they might be saved.

According to Pope Gregory, after new initiates and high-ranking witches had enjoyed a sumptuous banquet feast, they would all rise from the table as a black cat entered, walking backward with an erect tail. "First the novice kisses its hind parts," explains the treatise, "then the Master of Ceremonies proceeds to do the same and finally all the others in turn; or rather all those who deserve the honor." The lurid description continues:

> *When they have returned to their places they stand in silence for a few minutes with heads turned towards the cat. Then the Master says: "Forgive us." The person standing behind him repeats this and a third adds, "Lord we know it." A*

fourth person ends the formula by saying, "We shall obey."
When this ceremony is over the lights are put out and those
present indulge in the most loathsome sensuality, having
no regard to sex. If there are more men than women, men
satisfy one another's depraved appetites. Women do the
same for one another. When these horrors have taken place
the lamps are lit again and everyone regains their places.

The cat-as-Lucifer here lives up to contemporary #catsaresluts standards, first appearing as a symbol of arousal, then enticing folks to partake in the infamous analingual greeting witches were thought to use on the Devil (called *osculum infame*), and finally encouraging everyone to copulate with whom they pleased in a pansexual free-for-all.

This imagery was so awesome in the minds of a fearful populace that worshipping the Devil-as-cat in secret rites would be used to discredit various groups from the Waldensians and the Cathars to the Knights Templar. The hindquarter greeting would also play a part in rumors circulated about these Christian sects and later about witches.

Jean Tinctor's *Traittié du crisme de vauderie* painted between 1470 and 1480 in Bruges is a literal window into the practice. The circular pane set inside a square reveals five men in clerics' robes clustered around a cat's rear end. A horned Devil seems to goad them on as one man grasps a furry tail, about to raise it and bestow a greeting on the feline portal. The cat is not amused.

Vox in Rama helped lay the groundwork for the stigma not only against cats, but witches, too. According to historian Michael D. Bailey in the *Encyclopedia of Witchcraft: The Western Tradition*, the papal letter "marked an important step in the progressive demonization of heresy in the high and late Middle Ages that culminated in the notion of diabolical witchcraft."

In the years following its publication, a variety of social, cultural, religious, and economic factors coalesced to create what would become the early modern witch hunts, and it was during this period of great turmoil that witches, cats, and the Devil finally joined together in an unholy threesome that cast a long, dark shadow over Europe.

Death had claimed the cat. Up off the slick road a bloodied feline corpse was carried carefully, wet with tears and rain and mud, and buried deep in the sour ground. It would seem to be the end, but the sediment, the soil, the spirits forced life into that small body like so many blades of grass bursting from places they should not grow. What came after was another kind of cat, more prone to hissing, eyes glowing slime green, drunk on blood. In some ways it was more catlike than the cat it was before. The crouch, the yowl, the arch—these were the caustic calisthenics of a body possessed.

When the satanic word becomes flesh, the demonic often takes a feral, feline visage. The demon cat has no god and only some masters. We know these creatures from our folklore and from our films. They are harbingers. They circle the dead and the living. Sometimes, we make them into the demons they are, like Church, the cat described above from *Pet Sematary*, buried in a place he should not have been buried—then reanimated—and transformed from pet to pariah. In Stephen King's novel and film adaptation, human greed for life after life caused more heartache than relief.

But some demon cats needn't use humans to come back from the dead at all. The Japanese *nekomata*, the split-tailed cat, is said to be a necromancer. Only aged, large cats with long tails can transform into this type of powerful *yokai* who makes puppets of the dead. The *kasha*, in the same family, are also known for their corpse capers and drag body and soul to hell with them. Similarly, the Cat Sìth of Irish folklore—some say a fairy, some say a witch in a feline body—would leave a corpse, but steal a soul. Mourners had ways to distract this demon cat so they could stave off the soul-stealing with chants and games until burial.

Other demon cats are described as ghostly apparitions, like the one that haunts the United States Capitol Building. The *Washington Post* calls this "feline spook of the Capitol" "Washington's best ghost story" which dates back to the post-Civil War era. Spotted by security guards most notably before Lincoln and Kennedy were shot, the Demon Cat (shortened to D.C., natch) would supposedly catch you alone in a dimly lit hallway, then exponentially grow in size and attack. Like seeing the lion-headed chimera or the red-eyed cat called Cha Kla in Thai mythology, laying eyes on D.C. is—personally and politically—a bad omen.

Before we follow demon cats any further, it's essential to get our demonic history straight. What is a demon, and where do they originate?

There were plenty of malevolent spirits in ancient Mesopotamia and ancient Egypt, but the direct origin of the term *demon* can be traced back to the ancient Greek *daemon* or *daimon*, the word for a spirit or deity. There was no negative or evil implication in the original usage of this term. Instead, the daimon was a spirit guide who could influence a person's character or the outcome of a situation. Socrates believed his daimon positively helped him choose the right path in life, and later Aristotle would name the purpose of his ethical philosophy *eudaimonia*, which means "good spirit" or "happiness." The nature of the daimon morphed during the Hellenistic period to refer to two types of lesser spirits: noble spirits and malevolent spirits. After that, it was the Christians, always looking to discount the pagan past, who made demons fully diabolic.

By the Middle Ages, demons were an accepted part of life, writes Diana Lynn Walzel in *Sources of Medieval Demonology*. "Demons were part of the cosmic order (or disorder) and impinged on the world of everyone." They were also thought to change shape as they saw fit, "and most frequently they took on fantastic animal shapes." Walzel cites the Egyptians as the first culture to give demons animal form, even if they were not all considered evil. Later, the Romans would paint wild scenes of Diana, goddess of the moon, leading a horde of demon-animals on which humans would sometimes hitch a ride.

The "Savage Hunt of Heidesheim is known for its music, its wailing cats," writes Lotte Motz in "The Winter Goddess: Percht, Holda, and Related Figures."

"A church canon of the ninth century speaks in condemnation of women who assert that they had ridden out with a crowd of nocturnal 'demons,'" she continues, "and a sermon of the fifteenth century censures those who still believe that Diana, 'commonly known as fraw Percht,' is wont to wander through the darkness with her throng."

Gender, fundamentally, has little to do with these entities, although people do like to attribute gender to them. Many demonologists agree that demons can shape-shift to take any form they please and aren't hemmed in by our feeble binary. Nevertheless, history suggests that when you cross the demon feminine with the demon feline, the horror increases—at least for a male audience.

Lilith, one of the most infamous female demons, has been given top billing in Jewish demonic lore. Referenced in the *Epic of Gilgamesh* and likely related to the Mesopotamian female spirits known as *lilitu*, Lilith is first described as Adam's first wife in the satirical medieval work the *Alphabet of Ben Sira*. Because she refuses to submit sexually to her husband and shouts the forbidden name of God aloud, she screeches away and transforms into a vampiric succubus who copulates with angels, consumes children, and steals semen from men in their sleep so she can produce her demon offspring. She is known for her uncontrollable wantonness and her wrath. The Dead Sea Scrolls list her as a demon to take note of, and spells to protect against her dark doings have been found on Babylonian incantation bowls. Women would place amulets to ward off her presence when they were about to give birth. She was also known to take a feline form.

In medieval Spain, El Broosha or El Brooja (aka "witch" in Spanish) was a similar vampiric demon who was said to appear as a beastly black cat and drink the blood of babies. In Sephardic Jewish belief, this creature was Lilith incarnate, merely in feline skin. J. E. Hanauer recounts a tale told to him by a Spanish Jewish woman in *Folk-lore of the Holy Land* that new mothers would not leave the room with their newborn babies for nine days and nights until they could be sure El Broosha wasn't going to appear and snatch their child. Any appearance of a cat spelled trouble.

During the European witch hunts, it was widely held that demons could inhabit the bodies of animals, too, and many a witch fraternized with supernatural evil via goats, dogs, snakes, ravens, hogs, toads, and, of course, cats.

In 1318, Lady Alice Kyteler, Ireland's first accused witch, was said to have murdered her four previous husbands and communed with a demon who took the form of a cat. (She also possessed a trove of flying ointment which she *may* have rubbed on her nether regions to transcend this mortal coil.)

In 1320, Dante used a cat metaphor to describe demons overtaking newly damned sinners in hell. "The mouse had arrived among the she-cats," he writes in *The Divine Comedy*. (The Underworld may be led by a dark lord, but its bureaucracy is über-feminine.)

Fast-forward a few centuries to the late 1400s, and the *Malleus Maleficarum* linked lascivious witches and cats as an established part of Christian folk beliefs. Its chief author, a German Catholic friar named Heinrich Kramer, affirmed that the Devil would lead witches to change into many forms to do harm, and cats were one such glamour for they were "an appropriate symbol of the perfidious, just as a dog is the symbol of preachers; for cats are always setting snares for each other."

The *Malleus* was but one of many tracts that would "document" the perfidy and erotic proclivities of witches. Even though some scholars say it was outsized in its obscenity and woman-hating, it has nevertheless been cited as marking a shift in perceptions about witches. It did the same for cats.

In the medieval period, "cats were primarily associated with heretics and only rarely with witches," medieval historian Dr. Irina Metzler explains in an article about cats in the Middle Ages on her website. It was only toward the end of the medieval period that both witches and cats slowly transitioned from maligned but often ignored members of the community to the rot that must be rooted out to save it. "The pairing cat-witch is mainly a postmedieval phenomenon, as indeed the whole witch-craze and persecution of witches is an early modern rather than medieval episode," Metzler writes.

Inspired by the *Malleus Maleficarum* and similar witch-hunting works that followed, thousands of women (and many men) would be accused of and executed for practicing witchcraft, and countless cats would be beaten, hanged, drowned, and thrown from bell towers or into the flames of a pyre as a direct result of their association with witches, demons, and the Devil himself.

Twisted tales of feline diablerie only escalated as witch hysteria raged on.

Agnes Bowker said she had sex with the Devil in the form of a cat in 1560s London.

Janet Wishart and her witch accomplices of Aberdeen were accused of raising "nightmare cats" in 1597 to torment citizens in their sleep. (What "nightmare cats" are is lost in the annals of history, but what a delight to imagine.)

Dorothea Braun of Augsburg confessed in a 1625 interrogation that another witch attempted to school her in the ways of flying via feline, but the cat denied her the ride. (Anyone who has tried to *make* their cat do anything can surely sympathize.)

A German man named Viet Karg admitted to the authorities in 1680 that he had had sex with the Devil in female form with cloven hooves. He also said that the Devil appeared to him, among other things, as a cat.

Demons took different forms so frequently that early modern demonologists liked to debate why they were so fond of shape-shifting, historian of British folklore Ronald Hutton explains in *The Witch: A History of Fear, from Ancient Times to the Present*. "Nicholas Remy, in Lorraine, thought that there were practical reasons," Hutton writes. For example, "as cats, they could get into houses to work evil for their human allies." A French judge who instigated dozens of witch hunts, Pierre de Lancre, had other ideas, Hutton notes, and suggested that Satan was a "compulsive shapeshifter" because of his "general hatred of order and stability."

Whichever it is, individual tales of demonic cats and the Devil taking feline form are numerous across Western Europe, and in Poland, Croatia, and Italy, folk beliefs held that sorceresses would often take the form of cats, too. The idea of a cat familiar, however—or any kind of familiar at all—is a distinctly English phenomenon.

It was during the prosecution of witches in Chelmsford, England, in 1566 that demonic familiars were first documented in trial records, notes Brian P. Levack in *The Witchcraft Sourcebook*. "Familiars were minor demonic spirits that took the shapes of cats and other animals and were believed to assist witches in performing their malevolent magic," he explains. They likely arose out of ritual magic practices of centuries past, where "educated magicians claimed to be able to imprison imps in bottles or rings and then command them to perform magic," Levack writes.

In return for a little nourishment—blood, bodily fluids—suckled from a witch's teat—sometimes designated as the clitoris, sometimes a skin tag under the arms or a supernumerary nipple near the breasts—the familiars would do her bidding.

This symbiosis between witch and familiar not only mocked the sanctity of motherhood and its fluid bonds, but mirrored other kinds of ecstatic communion, too. "The witch embodied the misuse of the body, including her own; her familiars licking her body uncannily replicated pilgrims kissing and licking the grimy relics and icons of the pre-Reformation Church," Diane Purkiss suggests in "Witchcraft in Early Modern Literature."

Blurring the boundaries between animal and human, master and servant, the witch and her familiar would take up a vibrant role in witchy lore. But despite contemporary associations between the two, the majority of trial records do not reference animal familiars, writes Ronald Hutton. "Most English cases of witchcraft made no reference to them, but they were still prominent in an important minority, and especially in published accounts of trials, which helped to shape the image of witches in the public mind, and later in the minds of historians," he elucidates in *The Witch*.

When familiars were mentioned, however, they were often feline. "The familiars of Witches do most ordinarily appeare in the shape of cats, which is an argument that this beast is dangerous in soule and body," affirms Edward Topsell in *Historie of Fourefooted Beasts* from 1607.

Fifty years prior, Agnes Waterhouse, the first woman to be executed for witchcraft in England, admitted to being intimates with Satan—not the actual Devil, mind you, but a cat, whose name was Satan. She received the cat from another accused witch Elizabeth Francis, who had gotten the cat from her grandmother, who was also supposedly a witch.

Satan (also spelled as Sathan in a pamphlet from 1556) was a spotted white cat, and in exchange for a drop of blood, would do anything for its owner. Satan helped Francis induce an abortion by drinking herbs. Satan helped kill Francis's toddler. Satan helped Francis permanently disable her husband. Then, Francis traded Satan to Waterhouse for a delicious cake. Waterhouse, in turn, used Satan to decimate livestock, but was never able to murder anyone with Satan's powers.

In 1644, the most famous group of familiars materialized in a confession drawn out by English witchfinder general Matthew Hopkins. After days of torture, a local woman detailed her menagerie of animal cohorts, which included Holt, "who came in like a white kittling" (kitten). Holt may have been the first familiar, but there were also dogs, rabbits, polecats, and imps with names like Elemanzer, Pyewacket, Peckin the Crown, Grizzel, and Greedigut. Pyewacket would later become a common name for a cat familiar (made famous in 1958's *Bell, Book, and Candle*), but was not actually described as feline in the confession or the resulting woodcut featured on the front of Hopkins's 1647 pamphlet, *The Discovery of Witches*.

By the 1600s, ideas about witches and animal familiars had traveled across the Atlantic to infiltrate New England's colonies. The Massachusetts legal code established in 1641 included a proclamation about both witches and familiars, which would be used during the Salem trials to prosecute suspects. "If any man or woman be a witch (that is, hath or consulteth with a familiar spirit), they shall be put to death."

Tituba, a Barbadian woman enslaved by Reverend Samuel Parris, was one of the first three suspects arrested in Salem in 1692. In her confession, she revealed that the Devil did implore her to do his bidding, and that a variety of demonic animals appeared to her, including a red cat and a black cat who told her: "serve me."

The appearance of demonic cats in other Salem confessions would infuse them into American legend in the ensuing years. By the time the witch reached our screens, cats were a stock part of her story.

Feline Familiars

Spirits of the forest
I pronounce my intentions to thee
Come forth and seek me
And equal we will be
Not master and servant
But familiar to familiar
To share our knowledge
Our spirit and our traits
Now spirits, we will wait

Sabrina stands deep in the woods at twilight, speaking aloud a spell to find a familiar. Her aunts Zelda and Hilda have recently directed her to choose one from the registry book, offering her hedgehog, owl, or dog options, but she knows better. "I've been practicing a summoning spell I found in the Demonomicon," Sabrina counters. "What if I put it out there that I'm looking for a familiar and see if anyone wants to volunteer?"

In the first episode of *The Chilling Adventures of Sabrina*, the titular teenage witch stands in a scarlet coat with a bell in her hand, speaking aloud a verse that she hopes will call in her twin flame from the other realm. Less than a day later, her dark prayers are answered. Just out of the bath, she hears a noise in her room, and a tentacled vapor comes into view above her closet door.

"I heard you calling in the woods and I came," it whispers. The being disappears in a smoky puff and a small black cat pads forward with a trill. She grins. Sabrina's satanic meet-cute is finally happening. Salem, her familiar, has arrived to guide, protect, and aid her craft.

Familiar animals—felines in particular—are an elemental part of witchy tales. We are often privy to the ways familiars and their witches work magic in tandem. Seeing the initial, enchanted meeting between a witch and her magical partner—or at least one that is conjured up by a witch herself, as in the latest iteration of *Sabrina the Teenage Witch*—is rarer. Most often, we encounter a familiar who somehow finds its way to a witch, or a witchy woman who already has a cat and suddenly realizes that their connection is beyond the usual bond of pet and owner.

In the 1958 film *Bell, Book, and Candle*, sorceress Gillian Holroyd's Siamese cat Pyewacket has a purr and stare that help unlock her enchantments. When the witch locks eyes with Jimmy Stewart's character in a love spell, it is her familiar's magic that seems to put him over the edge (or maybe, her familiar's dander).

In Hayao Miyazaki's 1989 animated classic *Kiki's Delivery Service*, witch-in-training Kiki has a familiar named Jiji, a talking black cat who watches over her and fills in the blanks when her magic isn't quite up to snuff.

In the *Charmed* TV series from the late 1990s, the three Halliwell sisters have Kit, their feline guide sent to help them fulfill their magical destinies. Kit does this so well that she is blessed with a human form eventually, becoming Katrina.

Cat familiars are equally popular in literature.

The Cheshire Cat from *Alice's Adventures in Wonderland* is one of the most famous feline guides. Granted, Alice isn't often thought of as a witch, but she and the inimitable smiling pussy do have a familiar relationship. Alice comes upon the cat—or is it the cat who comes upon her?—and he opens ideological doors she never would have found without him. A shape-shifting trickster, the Cheshire Cat expands Alice's mind not only through his words but also through his malleability and vanishing act. He is undoubtedly an animal guide, and she has plenty of her own magical abilities, too.

Philip Pullman's *His Dark Materials* trilogy features daemons as spirit guides named after the ancient Greek guardian spirits. These familiars reflect attributes of a particular person, and so their shapes shift until that person has reached adulthood. The protagonist of the series, Lyra Belacqua, appears as part of a witches' prophecy, and has a daemon named Pantalaimon who sometimes takes the form of a wildcat.

J.K. Rowling's Harry Potter series also includes plenty of animal/witch relationships. The most prominent one is between the most industrious witch at Hogwarts School of Witchcraft and Wizardry, Hermione Granger, and Crookshanks, a bright-orange, lion-like cat. He can detect the unseen world with ease, letting Granger know when animals around her aren't what they seem.

Cats and witches have made an inseparable, iconic pair for so long that it's important to tease out fact from fiction. The early modern witch trials helped spread the idea of a pact between magical felines and wicked females in Euro-American lore, suffused with devious doings, fluid sharing, and all kinds of maleficium. There is, however, a less salacious kind of relationship that pervades contemporary occult communities. A far cry from the innocents who were accused of sorcery and witchcraft centuries ago, millions of people today self-identify as witches, pagans, neo-pagans, occultists, and intuitives—and also happen to work with an animal, often a cat, as an intimate part of their spiritual practice. From Wiccans and hoodoo and voodoo practitioners to kink witches, ceremonial magicians, and eclectic sorceresses, I interviewed dozens of women who positioned their feline(s) as an integral part of their magical identity.

Bri Luna, founder and visual director of *The Hoodwitch* and one of the most well-known proponents of modern witchcraft, views her cat as a pillar of her magical family. "He'll choose cards with his teeth when I'm doing readings," she laughs, "and he loves being part of rituals. He's part of everything I do," she tells me. "When I look into his eyes, I know he's magic."

After scouring Seattle for a Persian kitten, Luna was frustrated after meeting so many shady breeders. But with her intentions set, she soon stumbled upon a "super witchy, really spiritual woman" with wild red hair who would traverse the city streets with hand-raised Persians inside the basket of her bike. Luna visited this local witch (named Kitty, of course) at her Victorian home adorned with moon-shaped moldings. Before Kitty would let Luna take home the kitten that would become Klaus, she had to read her cards. "It was a really insightful reading," Luna recalls, and became a bonding moment between the women. Klaus immediately became an intimate in Luna's life, and the two remain inseparable. Every time Luna does a protection spell or a house blessing, he's a part of it.

In a book on familiar magic, Wiccan priest Raven Grimassi describes how a relationship with an animal familiar can be symbiotic. "Possessing a Familiar spirit allows the Witch to merge with the instincts of the animal and thereby interface with the *intelligence* of Nature," he writes in *The Witch's Familiar: Spiritual Partnership for Successful Magic*, noting that an animal's physical and psychic senses are stronger than humans. Grimassi continues: "The Familiar also benefits from having a relationship with the Witch," receiving "an expanded view of reality" which the animal can receive through this human intimacy.

Although no cats were available for comment (at least none that I could understand), the witches I spoke with about their feline familiars repeatedly referred to a closeness that seemed to benefit both beings in a multitude of ways.

Sybil J. describes her cat Shaolin as a healer who has seen her through both physical and metaphysical challenges. "She's very protective," Sybil says. "If I'm sick, she's lying on me." Despite Shaolin's witchy powers, however, she does have a distaste for incense and sage. "I always thought she was a little heathen," Sybil explains, but she then realized it might instead be the energies that are being chased away with incense and sage that her cat is sensitive to. "She's been through so much with me and my mom. She's like a spiritual guard cat."

Amy M. finds similar support from her black cat Walter, who came into her life as a kitten rescued from the New York City subway. "I think he helps me in emotional ways. I talk to him a lot; we have a special, very close bond. You could call it a spiritual connection," she muses.

Sandra R. calls her cat Pumpkin, "an incredibly special animal." Years ago, when she was planning on adopting a cat for Christmas, she got into a cab on December 20, and the driver offered her his cat, which he needed to rehome. "Of all the taxicabs that I could have taken that night, it seems incredibly serendipitous that I, who wanted a cat, would happen to get into the cab whose driver had a cat who needed a home," she exclaims. "Hands down the best manifestation I could have ever conjured!" Since that time, their relationship has only deepened. "I don't know if he is my familiar or my soul mate," Sandra says. "I truly believe he has helped pull me through some of the worst times, be it by absorbing some of my negative energy or simply providing warmth and love when I needed it most, and I am incredibly thankful to him for that."

Although not all witches I interviewed were intentional about including their feline partners in their rituals, dozens of practitioners said their cats were naturally curious and loved being around them while lighting candles, pulling cards, or meditating.

"She just likes to do everything with me, so this is an extension of our relationship," Sarah P. says about her cat. "She engages with my spells, crystals, cards. She really loves sigil magic, and I believe she has imparted her own magic onto them before they are burned. She completely involves herself in a way that lets me know, 'hey, I am part of this too, obviously.'"

Vanessa I. reveals that since she adopted her cat Belladonna, her life and her witchcraft have changed for the better. "I feel like I've become more open emotionally and spiritually than I was before," she explains. "I'm softer (and harder) in different places now, and it's absolutely affected my practice. She's always curious about what I'm working on and loves to hang around my altars. When I talk to my ancestors, she will meow along. I have a small statue of Bast now that I placed a bit of her fur on to watch out for her and keep her safe. I'm pretty sure she brought some friends as well because I see them out of the corner of my eye constantly now. I had no idea how special and magical having a cat would be, and I honestly don't know how I ever lived without her," Vanessa says.

"I consider my cat a partner in my own offshoot of nonpracticing Sufism," Leila J. tells me. "I grew up as many Muslims have, considering cats 'clean' animals because their cleansing rituals are similar to that of a human's and hearing tales of how cats can view fire elementals/djinns. I still believe that they can lift the veil between our world and others, see what isn't there, and sense emotions," she continues. Although Leila doesn't use the term *familiar* to describe their relationship, her cat does join her during meditation. "She's most enamored by the breathing exercise of the *dzikir*, and I think of us breathing as one if she's in my lap," she says.

Other witches have expressed a deep psychic connection with their cats. Suzy M.'s cat has joined her through "multiple psychic travels" and acted as a grounding force. "She communicates with me. I give her love and luxury and protection. She gets safety, although as a house cat, I feel sad for her stunted instincts. Trade-offs. But I do feel we were meant to be together in this life," she concludes.

Lia De O.'s witchcraft practice as a dominant includes cathartic BDSM rituals, and she considers her two cats familiars and healers. "Lucy basically only takes care of me when I suffer from dom drop, which is the cutest thing ever," she notes, "while Lily is all the way there for my bottoms, snuggling them, meowing . . . bringing them back to the ground in the most loving way."

Luna D., a self-described intuitive and medium for the Dark Goddess archetype, was very open about the alliance she has with her cat Sarah. "She appears in my dreams regularly as a trigger to lucid dreaming where we can talk more clearly, and she tells me about her adventures or how she feels about my sadness. I admire the wild wisdom about her and she trusts me completely," Luna says. "I've been a lucid dreamer since I can remember," she elaborates. "I have created tools to help me understand what my unconscious mind is working through such as learning the tarot symbolism, studying the works of people like Carl Jung, and since her birth, Sarah. She has greater access to a world I'm not as familiar with, but I'm increasingly aware that the origins of archetypes come from the ancient patterns evolving in nature. She has brought the joy of Bast into my life."

Like cultural ideas about the witch, the concept of a familiar has gone through an arduous rehabilitation process since the early modern witch trials. Today, the evil aura surrounding the witch-familiar relationship has all but dissolved, but a mystical intimacy remains.

"Creatures of such deep attachment we call our familiars—animals who, in some way, are linked to the very fiber of our being," Alexis Palmer Karl writes in a piece about familiars for *Venefica* magazine. Karl terms this bond "a connection that confounds the modern understanding of friendship as defined through the filter of relentless social media . . . for it is in the slow gaze of an animal that we might see our own true reflection."

As beautiful as it may be, such close companionship with an animal isn't regarded with much esteem in Western culture. And women—regardless of magical affiliation—have been particularly stigmatized for seeing their true reflection in cats.

The Cat Lady—Crazy, Sexy, Queer

At eight years old, Eleanor Abernathy clutched her books to her chest, eyes wide and determined, and confessed her career aspirations. "I want to be a lawyer and a doctor because a woman can do anything," she chirped.

At twenty-four, Eleanor graduated from Harvard Law and Yale School of Medicine, with the world at her feet.

At thirty-two, alone and exhausted from years spent wading through the shards of a glass ceiling at which she had hammered away, Eleanor turned to alcohol—and her cat—for comfort.

At forty, Eleanor was no longer speaking in full sentences. She screamed unintelligible fragments at strangers in the street, her gray hair tangled, eyes wild. She owned more cats than anyone could count. Eleanor Abernathy had reached peak crazy cat lady.

So goes the backstory of one of TV's most recognizable caricatures of cat ownership. Up until Season 18 of *The Simpsons*, Abernathy was a nameless eccentric, known for a gravity-defying crown

of unkempt hair, a penchant for aggressive, incomprehensible solil-
oquies, and hurling cats at passersby. When the "Springfield Up"
episode finally deigned to give the Crazy Cat Lady a backstory, it
took the cliched narrative to the extreme.

The archetypal cat lady is the epitome of pathologized, heterosexual singlehood. She is a spinster, a hoarder, mentally ill. She's a failed
woman who misdirects her maternal instincts to dote on animals
who couldn't possibly love her back. For years, men have mocked
her, and women have clung to whatever relationship options they've
been afforded so they won't become her. And cats? Cats unwittingly
play the role of boyfriend, husband, and romantic surrogate.

When Kinneret Lahad explores felines and female singles in
*A Table for One: A Critical Reading of Singlehood, Gender, and
Time*, she suggests that "the presence of cats has come to symbolize
the lack of men in single women's lives, as by this point in their
lives they only have cats to keep them company." She adds: "this
could be seen as a metaphorical representation of the inferior status bestowed upon single women by society at large."

Devaluing women without male partners is nothing new. In fact,
cultures around the world have made old maids monstrous. Rangda,
the hideous, child-eating Balinese witch, is a vicious spinster whose
name literally means "widow" in Old Javanese. Yamauba, the
flesh-eating Japanese mountain crone, is a woman scorned.

But perhaps being single isn't the only reason cat ladies are
viewed with such derision in society. "The cat lady is distinct
from the spinster," posits Lila S., creator of the Litter app, a space
for feline adoration, cats, and cat devotees. "She has a nurturing
instinct that she is 'wasting' on animals instead of raising babies.
Cat ladies are despised more because they're failed mothers than
failed wives, neglecting not only to serve a husband, but to birth
and raise men."

Childless women, along with older, single, or widowed women, were most vulnerable to accusations of witchcraft in early modern Europe. As Pam Grossman writes in *Waking the Witch: Reflections on Women, Magic, and Power,* although witch hysteria has since died down, "the image of the monstrous antimother is still with us. Even today, in this age of 'you do you' self-actualization, the choice to not even *try* to have children is met with suspicion. *Selfish, damaged, stunted, too career-focused*—whatever the descriptors, the implication is that a woman who doesn't want children is somehow deficient and therefore destructive."

We know from chapter 3 that cats were one of the animals frequently associated with supposed witches, thought to be either their familiars or their feline forms. The cat lady can thus be viewed as an offshoot of the archetypal witch, who represents the ultimate perversion of Christian womanhood. The cat lady, however, is a softened trope, fit for the age of reason and beyond. Really, the way patriarchal society degrades women and their cats has merely changed shape. It's just an old prejudice with a new look.

The cat lady as a cultural figure arguably stretches back even before the witch trials, though, when felines were commonly kept by nuns—another icon of childless, female singlehood. An early thirteenth-century guide to monastic duties, *Ancrene Wisse,* allowed for women of the cloth to only keep cats—as long as they weren't too distracting. "Now if someone needs to keep [a cat], let her see to it that it does not annoy anyone or do any harm to anybody, and that her thoughts are not taken up with it," the text decreed. "An anchoress ought not to have anything which draws her heart outward."

The kind of cat lady we know and love/loathe today first began to appear in the eighteenth century, however. John Petit's engraving *Old Maids at a Cat's Funeral* from 1789 is a particularly solemn take. Eleven women stand amid a graveyard, all but one holding a cat. Two of them carry a tiny coffin painted with a small feline face. The only woman without a cat in her arms dabs a kerchief to her eye, gazing wistfully at the vessel holding her dearly departed pet.

By the time J.S. Neish had published *In the By-ways of Life: A Series of Sketches of Forfarshire Characters* nearly a century later in 1881, feline-female relationships were already subjects of ridicule. "Old maids and cats have long been proverbially associated together," Neish explains in his book about Scottish people, "and rightly or wrongly these creatures have been looked upon with a certain degree of suspicion and aversion by a large proportion of the human race." He then adds sympathetically that the association has been harsh, if not unfair. "Solitude is not congenial to human nature, and a poor forlorn female, shut up in a cheerless 'garret,' brooding all alone over her blighted hopes, would naturally centre her affections on some of the lower animals, and none would be more congenial as a pet and companion than a kindly purring pussy, with its sleek silky hair and velvet paws," Neish writes.

The author isn't so sympathetic that he can't resist telling the supposedly true story of Water Betty, though. An "odd-looking" woman who wore the "quaint dress of by-gone times," Betty delivered water for a living and so gained the nickname. She rescued cats of all breeds and ages, feeding them home-cooked meals, tending to them when they fell ill, and even designating separate living quarters for them. But Betty's "monomania for cats" would eventually be her undoing. The townspeople cared not for her unsightly home filled with feline friends and had them all massacred by police dogs, leaving Betty heartbroken and alone.

Most cat ladies in popular culture are mere caricatures designed to inspire revulsion or ridicule, however, not real people like Water Betty. The infamous 1975 documentary *Grey Gardens* is one exception, and arguably a crown jewel in the genre. The film follows two aging socialites from former First Lady Jackie Kennedy's clan who live in the literal ruins of their former glory. Stalking the property of the mother-daughter duo's decaying East Hampton estate are dozens of felines with names like Bigelow and Tedsy Kennedy (named because of a robust profile shared with the senator). In one scene, Big Edie (real name Edith Ewing Bouvier Beale) laughs when a cat pees on a portrait of her younger self, and in video footage from the *Grey Gardens* prequel, *That Summer*, Little Edie (real name Edith Bouvier Beale) notes that Tedsy isn't feeling well lately because she herself has been "very upset." No one is well in the house—not least because the health department has issued ultimatums to the women about cleaning up their trash-strewn home and bringing it up to code—or risk eviction.

What is different about the Edies from the typical cat lady narrative is that they are a *pair* of cat ladies. According to sexist norms, however, because they don't have romantic relationships with men, they remain alone and pitiful in the one sense that counts. Add this to their hoarding and cat loving and visible signs of mental illness and they check all the boxes.

The 1992 black comedy *Death Becomes Her* also played upon the frightening (this time fictional) extremes of the crazy cat lady trope. After Goldie Hawn's character Helen Norman is dumped by her fiancé for a glamorous actress played by Meryl Streep, her life spirals out of control. The depth of Norman's despair is demonstrated in a scene where Hawn wears an offensive fat suit while sitting and eating vanilla frosting with her hands surrounded by trash and a cluster of cats. Hypnotized by the TV, Norman obsessively rewatches scenes of her nemesis being strangled on screen as her landlord attempts to break down the door to collect back rent. To be fat, to be jilted, to have multiple cats, to display marked signs of neuroatypical behavior: these are the bogeymen that lurk for women who don't follow the patriarchally prescribed path.

Before we plunge deeper into cat lady land, it's important to note that societal views of cat-loving women may be rooted in sexism, but there is also the uncomfortable reality of cat hoarding. Animal hoarding is defined by the Anxiety and Depression Association of America as "the compulsive need to collect and own animals for the sake of caring for them that results in accidental or unintentional neglect or abuse." The ADAA notes that 70 percent of animal hoarders who have run-ins with the authorities are single, widowed, and divorced women. On the organization's website, the phrase "crazy cat lady" looms large before a description of the emotional life of hoarders:

> *Studies of animal hoarders show that their behavior often begins after an illness, disability or death of a significant other, or other difficult life event. They view their animals as a major source of love, and they emphasize how much they give and receive from them. For many, keeping their animals appears to guarantee a conflict-free relationship. They often refer to their animals as their babies, and they confuse their loving the animals with the reality of their inability to provide a safe, clean, and healthy home for them.*

The majority of this framework could be applied to many people who are fiercely devoted to their pets. However, there is a difference between hoarding and adoring your cats. Herein lies the problem with the crazy cat lady or cat lady stereotype, where someone with severe mental illness keeping numerous cats in unsafe and unsanitary conditions is conflated with someone who cherishes her pets and might even prefer their company to that of other humans.

There is also the idea, expressed in a variety of media—a gendered comedy trope, if you will—that one cat is a gateway drug to cat hoarding if you're a single woman of a certain age. You know the urban legend, about dying in your apartment alone, your body undiscovered for days as your cat feasts on your remains? The threat of pathologized singlehood coupled with the serious mental illness of hoarding is dangled as a cautionary tale for women so they straighten up and fly (marry and procreate) right.

Sometimes, though, cat ladies do get their due. In lighter, more humorous depictions, cat ladies have found a home on the small screen. *Are You Being Served*'s Mrs. Slocombe was always going on about her "pussy" to the great confusion of her coworkers, and *The Office*'s Angela Martin was once caught grooming one of her many cats with her tongue. These women had similar prim demeanors with a streak of wildcat that always shone through. As it turned out, Mrs. Slocombe enjoyed the attention of rough men at bars, and Angela had multiple suitors duel over her affections. Their cat ownership, even if portrayed as extreme, wasn't only about their perpetual singlehood; it was also about their hidden animal magnetism.

Recently, an episode of the musical dramedy *Crazy Ex-Girlfriend* covered the cat lady trope. The protagonist Rebecca Bunch, a young, professional lawyer who is diagnosed with borderline personality disorder, sings an entire song—complete with feline puppets!—about quitting the world of dating and getting a "Buttload of Cats." It's all very tongue in cheek, so the depiction welcomes knowing laughter as Bunch reveals her life path is so much clearer now that she's leaned into singlehood. "When you're a permanent bachelorette, it's mandatory that you go out and get a buttload of cats," she sings in a line with her best female friends, pawing at the air.

Bunch then heads to a mock pet store packed with cat puppets and single women. We're introduced to the proprietor of the place, dressed in a floral vest, and another customer in an "I love chocolate" shirt. Mid-conversation about their pets, the singletons bond as they open their wallets and dozens of cat photos in plastic sleeves accordion out onto the floor. Then, the cats in cages begin to sing about their woes, bemoaning the fact that felines have become inexorably linked to solitude and despair. Bunch finishes the song with a dramatic flourish on the topic of *Toxoplasma gondii,* a parasite found in cat feces, and how it reportedly makes you crazy. Regardless, she wants a buttload of cats.

The explicit link between mental illness and cats Bunch references in song has made headlines over the past fifteen years with the discovery of the toxoplasma pathogen. In a 2012 article in *The Atlantic* titled "How Your Cat Is Making You Crazy," author Kathleen McAuliffe explores the research of one Czech scientist, Jaroslav Flegr, who found that humans infected with *Toxoplasma gondii* can experience far-reaching side effects. By acting like a "microscopic puppeteer capable of pulling our strings," the organism "rewires circuits in parts of the brain that deal with such primal emotions as fear, anxiety, and sexual arousal."

Because *Toxoplasma gondii* can only reproduce in feline digestive tracts, the parasite's raison d'être is to get back inside a cat. Simply put, "the parasite has evolved a complicated system for taking over its hosts' brains to increase the likelihood that they'll be eaten by cats," explains Rebecca Skloot in her *New York Times* piece, "The 'Cat Lady' Conundrum." This is one explanation for why some people are so incredibly drawn to them.

"The rise of cats as pets, in fact, closely parallels the rise of insanity," writes E. Fuller Torrey in his book *The Invisible Plague:*

The Rise of Mental Illness from 1750 to the Present. There have been multiple studies, he explains, that link childhood exposure to cats with schizophrenia and manic depression. However, he cautions against going too far with this theory, as there are plenty of other hypotheses which account for why mental illness has increased exponentially in our society, from changes in diet and our environment to new infectious diseases.

When toxo expert Robert Sapolsky was asked in Skloot's 2007 *Times* article if there was a link between crazy cat ladies and this protozoan, he said, "That idea doesn't seem completely crazy. . . . But there's no data supporting it."

Still, toxoplasmosis has been unscientifically designated "crazy cat lady syndrome," and the way the general public views it (as evidenced by the *Crazy Ex-Girlfriend* song at least) is rife with assumptions.

New findings about *Toxoplasma gondii* make it easier to pathologize cat ladies, but there is concurrently a trend of young women reclaiming the cat lady moniker with a feminist twist, disavowing the "crazy" part altogether. Since both terms have been used interchangeably, creating a reliable taxonomy of cat ladydom is tricky, but necessary.

On the one hand, the crazy cat lady is no different than the cat lady. The former just includes an added descriptor that reveals deep-rooted prejudices up front instead of implying them. On the other hand, the crazy cat lady is more often depicted as suffering from a variety of mental health issues and reveals not only the extent of the stigma against neuroatypical people but also the stigma against single women with cats. By comparison, the cat lady is generally more benign, but viewed with similar disdain. She's quirky, lonely, a bit pathetic. The only romantic attention she's supposedly worthy of is from her cats.

If millions of Americans are infected with a mind-altering organism that can make them attracted to cats—the CDC puts the number at over sixty million—the difference between cat ladies and crazy cat ladies is subjective. Who's to say what's "crazy"? With so many well-publicized studies pathologizing cat ladies, it's important to look at research that shows why cats themselves might be drawn to women. One 2011 study published in the journal *Behavioural Processes* suggests that the attraction between the two may actually be reciprocal.

After 120 hours of following 40 cat-human couplings, researchers found that cats tended to favor the attention of female owners. Coauthor of the study Manuela Wedl of the University of Vienna said: "Cats approach female owners more frequently, and initiate contact more frequently (such as jumping on laps) than they do with male owners." She concluded that this was no coincidence, and that "female owners have more intense relationships with their cats than do male owners." This observation reflects the findings of an older study published in *Anthrozoös* that women were more likely to take on a more active role with their cats and thus experienced more frequent "approaches and withdrawals" than did male owners. A similar study of 157 Hungarian cat owners published in *Applied Animal Behaviour Science* found that women were more likely to find their cats "communicative and empathetic," which expressed itself in female owners talking and smiling to their cats more than male owners did. (In case you're wondering, the sex of the cat itself did not have a marked impact on these behavioral patterns.)

The sample sizes of these studies are small, which makes it unwise to put forth any blanket statements about the female-feline connection. Still, the results are telling. Not only is it apparent that female owners might indulge their cats more and thus receive a better response than male owners, it's also worth noting that there are few studies in which one can even explore the subject in depth. Cat research is far less common than, say, dog research—so much so that the inequity was the topic of a 2018 *New York Times* article.

When asked why she believed dogs were favored in research over cats, Dr. Elinor Karlsson, a geneticist at the Broad Institute and the University of Massachusetts said that "research has lagged behind in cats. I think they're taken less seriously than dogs, probably to do with societal biases." Animal cognition researcher Felicity Muth doesn't buy this assertion and wrote in *Scientific American*: "Cats are generally less cooperative and more nervous in social situations, meaning it's difficult to use them in experiments." Still, other scientists concurred with Karlsson that cultural views about cats are worth acknowledging—along with a variety of other biological and behavioral factors.

It doesn't take a geneticist to make the next logical leap. The idea of cats as less worthy of serious study is no doubt tied up in their centuries-old association with another similarly devalued attribute: femininity.

This leaves us pretty much back where we started. Science, like culture at large, isn't immune to the misogynistic mind-sets that continue to propagate stigma against single women and their cats. But thanks to feminist and queer theory, there is a way out of this mess. It only requires removing men from the equation entirely.

"This is Pearl," says comedian Kate McKinnon, gingerly lifting a white cat. As the purveyor of *Whiskers R We*, McKinnon's character Barbara DeDrew is desperate to entice adoption prospects. "Pearl is white as a ghost because she is one. She died in the 1940s but she's sticking around because she has unfinished business." "If she appears in your mirror, it's over!" quips McKinnon's "friend" played by Kristen Wiig. The audience ripples with laughter.

"This is Dizzy," continues Wiig, as she hoists a black and white kitten from the crate. "Dizzy is into S&M," she pauses, her adult braces causing a lisp. "Saucers and milk!"

"And also peeing on her partner during sex!" adds McKinnon with a devilish grin. (Most feline backstories in this recurring *Saturday Night Live* skit are equally absurd.)

Reveling in cringeworthy cat puns and hot female-on-feline action, Barbara DeDrew's job is getting cats and kittens adopted, but it's made near impossible by the roving hands of her flirty assistants. Played by Kristen Wiig, Charlize Theron, Amy Adams, Tiffany Haddish, and Melissa McCarthy in different episodes, these "friends" are Barbara's many admirers who alternately annoy her and arouse her on camera as they fondle her arms, breasts, and butt suggestively while she tries to rehome the cats in her charge.

"Keep it in your jorts, GF!" Barbara barks as Wiig, unable to keep her hands to herself, paws at McKinnon.

At first glance, the women of *Whiskers R We* are your typical cat ladies, embodying clichés that have been circulating since Water Betty. Think out-of-fashion outfits like mom jeans, braided belts, and Laura Ashley florals, awkward body language, and nary a husband in sight. However, the women of *Whiskers R We* and the previously discussed cat ladies diverge at a critical juncture. Barbara DeDrew and her friends aren't pitiable, but in their sexual prime. They don't give a damn about how they look to men or about men at all. It's not the male gaze that dictates how they live their lives—it's the meow gaze.

Queer women and cats are still in the midst of a torrid love affair. Their association can be traced back at least to the witch hunts, when images of naked women cavorting together often featured cats, demonizing nonnormative sex and warning the populace about the perils of witchcraft in one fell swoop. Sapphic symbology was endemic to witchcraft in the early modern era as tales of witches in feline form and feline demons spread across Europe. However, it would be missing the mark to attribute this pairing solely to the patriarchs.

In an article for *The Cut*, "'Cat Knows How to Ignore Men': A Brief History of Lesbian Cat Ladies," Nicole Pasulka tackles the cult of felines and queer femininity. "Most women assiduously avoid the 'cat lady' label, but lesbians have embraced the association," she explains. "While the rest of the world cringed and laughed, this stereotype of fierce love for cats has helped queer and gay women build community and visibility for nearly 50 years." She not only cites *Whiskers R We*, but lesbian periodicals from the 1970s, the 1991 anthology *Cats (and Their Dykes)*, and the 2016 book *The Lesbian Sex Haiku Book (With Cats!)* as touchstones in this storied history. Witches are also part of the equation. "Wicca and witchcraft—which have featured cats as companions in spiritual matters and in persecution for hundreds of years—appeal to women generally disgusted by the demands of marriage, gender roles, or mainstream femininity," Pasulka writes.

Women who consorted with animals and cared not for the company of men could easily have been accused of witchcraft in centuries past. Nowadays, women who fail to fall in line with compulsory heterosexuality can face similar persecution, but in many circles are lauded for living life on their own terms. In that sense, the queer cat lady has become a liberating archetype.

Capturing this spirit in sonic form is the 2015 song "Kittenz," delivered with tongue-in-cheek bombast by Sapphic Musk. The L.A.-based band describes its music as "Sapphic warrior rock from Lezstonia" and created an internet sensation with the music video for this headbanger. Drawing from Viking mythology and hard rock aesthetics, frontwoman Sara T. Russell belts her heart out into the mic: "To the mighty paw I bow down low / Siamese, Tabby, Calico / Claws like demon knives / They don't die they've got nine lives" as kittens crowd-surf and wreak havoc backstage. Cats harbor a mysterious magic, the song tells us, as the riffs and intensity crescendo into the chorus: "Kittens to the left of me, kittens to the right, kittens in the back of me, every freakin' night!"

These aren't the dowdy charmers of *Whiskers R We;* these tough-as-leather dykes have axes to grind and stages to conquer.

In an interview with the *Huffington Post*, singer-songwriter Russell, fully aware of the lesbian cat cliché, admitted that the song was poking fun at the band members. "It's about laughing at ourselves," she explained. Only a group of queer women versed in the occult-loving genre of heavy metal would be fit to aurally transmit the power and glory of cats.

This intersection between cats, queer women, and the occult has rarely been studied seriously, but there are plenty of informal stats to make up for it. Autostraddle, the world's most popular lesbian website (which, incidentally, has a self-appointed cat editor), published the Lesbian Stereotypes Survey in 2018 with a post titled "It's True: Queer Women Own the Most Cats."

Over 12,000 LGBTQ+ women and nonbinary people responded to the digital questionnaire, and 43 percent identified themselves as cat owners. That's a noticeable difference compared to 36 percent of all Americans who own cats, according to a recent national pet owners survey. But that's just the beginning. Five percent of those surveyed by Autostraddle identified as pagan, Wiccan, or as a witch, compared to 0.3 percent who identified as the same in a 2014 Pew Religious Landscape Study of 35,000 Americans. And as far as cat-owning queer women go, they are 23 percent more likely to practice witchcraft than dog-owning queer women.

Autostraddle also found out the following fascinating tidbits:

Cat owners are more likely than dog owners to be vegan (6 percent), identify as hard femme (7.5 percent), be trans (which includes nonbinary people) (28 percent), be queer-identified (29.5 percent), have an undercut (20 percent), not remove any body hair (11 percent), have long nails (8.6 percent), use menstrual cups (29 percent), have complete confidence in their sewing abilities (48 percent), read their horoscopes regularly (23.4 percent), be an unaffiliated atheist (25 percent), do at least some witchcraft (23 percent), have gone to a women's college (7 percent), and to prefer nonmonogamy (22.4 percent).

This deep dive into the minutiae of cat-owning queer folks is fascinating, but generalizations about queer cat ladies are equally important to analyze, too. The "I think I'm queer" starter pack meme posted by @memesforvalidation features, among other things, a pair of combat boots, an *L Word* promo shot, and a picture of a cat.

Lesbian meme queen @xenaworrierprincess posted a meme describing a "Successful Lesbian Date," which includes talking about food allergies and sharing parts of your life story, such as coming out and "significant cats."

And go to any site targeting queer women or lesbians and you'll find article titles like "10 Lesbians And Their Gorgeous Cats" (*Go Magazine*); "9 Reasons Lesbians and Cats Are Perfect Together" (AfterEllen), and "5 Ways Lesbians Are Just Like Cats" (Pride).

Serious literary efforts are just as likely to tackle this alliance as lesbian listicles are. Renowned poet, activist, and womanist Audre Lorde writes plenty about her beloved felines and is even called "slick kitty from the city" by her first female lover in her 1982 autobiography *Zami: A New Spelling of My Name*.

In Leslie Feinberg's groundbreaking genderqueer novel *Stone Butch Blues*, one of the protagonist's femme lovers, Milli, is symbolized by a porcelain kitten figurine keepsake.

And in radical punk writer Kathy Acker's correspondence collection with McKenzie Wark, *I'm Very Into You: Correspondence 1995–1996*, she writes: "I have about a hundred cats living in me and all of them are curious."

None of the above queer cat media is derogatory in the slightest. Queer cat ladies, unlike their heterosexual counterparts, face far less derision. In fact, there is a pervasive sentiment that if you are a lesbian or a queer woman and *don't* like cats, you're going to run into trouble.

Take, for example, Krista Burton's opinion piece for the *New York Times*: "I'm a Lesbian Who Hates Cats. I'm Going to Die Alone." The author describes her list of "relationship deal breakers" that happen to include owning a cat. Her friend, upon reading the list, said that her dating days are numbered. "Do you know who mostly owns cats? Women. Queers," she asserts. "Not all women, and not all queers, obviously, but go on, I dare you—try being queer and hating cats and looking online for dates. So many queers on Tinder or Her or OkCupid are obsessed with their cats. Sometimes they will post pictures of their cats as their only profile picture," she continues, or, if they don't, they'll show you pictures of their cat on a first date, at least.

So why do queer women dedicate themselves so heartily to the feline kind? It's pure masochism, Burton suggests, because women and queers have "been conditioned to love and perform labor for creatures that don't necessarily love us back, care about our needs and may even wish us ill. Like women loving cis men."

Burton's spin is that cats are indeed a perfect stand-in for cisgender, heterosexual men because of their propensity for ghosting, for ungrateful responses to heartfelt care, and for general selfishness. But such is a cynical read on cat-woman relationships. One could easily argue that cats will never cheat on you. They will be dedicated to you until they die. They have access to other kinds of consciousness that cis men only dare dream to achieve. And it is this perspective that has driven contemporary cat ladies of the queer and straight variety to proudly own their feline obsessions.

Centuries after accused witches confessed to having cat familiars, old maids wept at a cat's funeral, and Water Betty was ostracized because of her feline caretaking, women are still fighting to wrest the cat lady stereotype off their backs. BriAnne Wills, a New York City-based photographer, is one such woman, who created the series "Girls and Their Cats" in 2015 after her own experiences with cat lady stigma.

"I knew that cat ladies were more than what they were portrayed as in the media," Wills tells me one afternoon over the din of a Brooklyn café. But it wasn't until she was shooting a nude photo series of women in their homes that something clicked. "I thought I would bring in a different perspective, being a female photographer, like, let's see the female gaze on naked women," she explains. "Nothing was sexual about [the model] being naked. She was just a naked woman in her home," Wills adds.

And then something unexpected happened. Curious about what was going on, the model's cat jumped into the mix, and Wills kept on taking pictures of the pair. "The cat comes in, and she's a naked woman in her home with her cat. That was it. I started taking photos of them together and that's when the lightbulb moment happened."

Four years and over 280 cat ladies later, Wills is still documenting women in their homes with the cats they have rescued, standing by her "adopt don't shop" ethos. "The only goal I really set out to achieve was to show that the cat lady is so many different types of women," she says. "That's it. The only commonality we have and we can find is our love for our cats."

Wills pauses and admits there might actually be one thing they all share. "Every woman I photograph is doing something cool with her life," Wills smiles.

In 2019, she gathered some of her favorite features into a book about the series, also called *Girls and Their Cats*. It's a timely endeavor, particularly as women's bodily autonomy remains a subject of debate in the political sphere. "It's all related," Wills says. "Cats have also gotten a bad rap on their own without being connected to women. There's that connection between being independent and not wanting to be tied down by anything," she explains. "Body autonomy. Cats understand consent and boundaries. And I think they can teach us about that as well."

Other media outlets are also waving the furry feminine flag. *Refinery 29* attempted to reframe perceptions about the cat lady with the digital feature "Modern Day Cat Ladies."

"I own it: I'm a cat lady, I don't care, I have no shame," says one young woman, "I am all about this lifestyle. . . . What attracted me to cats is that they're self-sufficient, just like how I'm trying to be."

"I think the modern cat lady can do it all," says another woman, holding her cat. "I think she can be a boss at work, but I also think a cat lady can be super maternal and loving and know that when she comes home she's gonna have these cute little critters to take care of and they're gonna love her back."

The cat lady stereotype can be used to explore not only the ways male-dominated society perceives women, but also how women perceive themselves. In this sense, inhabiting the cat lady stereotype—or, more positively put, the cat lady archetype—allows women to subvert their relationship with gender norms and expectations.

In an essay published in the *Midway Review*, Breck Radulovic argues that lesbian cat ladies are particularly radical because they challenge the hierarchy inherent in patriarchy. "By forming relationships with cats through affection, companionship, and direct association, lesbians dissolve the anthropocentrism at the heart of heteropatriarchy, and in doing so queer it profoundly."

This perspective is a powerful one, but perhaps it can be expanded to further the destruction of hegemonic norms. If dominion over all species—including women—is what animates patriarchy, an equal relationship with a cat, or any animal, is inherently anti-patriarchal. Because femininity—and animals—are so devalued, disregarded, and infantilized in our culture, perhaps any person on the feminine spectrum, cis or trans, gay or straight, can challenge male and masculine hegemony through unabashedly pledging feline allegiance. If this is the case, then conscious connection with our animal allies is a necessity for feminist action. And a legion of young women and queer folks are discovering and committing to this practice, one cat at a time.

Cats, Kink, and Kitten Play

I ran my unmanicured fingers purposefully through the racks. Buckles, o-rings, and zippers collided, plastic hangers swayed. The corseted salesgirl shot me a look as the row of fetish gear trembled with the aftershock of my nervous inertia. She seemed to recognize me from other times I had come in to peruse the latex, never buying, but trying it on—or pretending to—because I had no idea what to do with the bottle of talcum powder she handed me before I went into the dressing room.

Six years after *Batman Returns* confirmed my kink curiosities, I was ready to level up. Inside Dream Dresser, an adult boutique just off the waterfront in Washington D.C.'s tony Georgetown neighborhood, cats stalked the aisles. Patent leather catsuits called to me. Cheap fuzzy cat ears blurred the lines between novelty and kink. Cat masks invoked a boudoir masquerade. The tangled tentacles of cat-o'-nine-tails hung in repose. All these cats and more were native to my slice of BDSM paradise. And though some pieces could undoubtedly be used for an upgraded Catwoman costume, even in my naivete I knew they were meant for *something else*.

Desperate to cross the boundary between proper and perverse (and to skin the cat that was my virginity), I intuited that acting more catlike, more like the animals that shared my bed and seemed to come and go as they pleased, was the way to go. I was already well-equipped for crossing the boundaries between animal and human from my forays into celluloid cosplay. So armed with my pristinely kept copies of *Skin Two* and *Marquis*, the only fetish magazines I could find to guide me, I set out to understand more of myself through a forbidden world.

To uncover the erotics of the animal kingdom is to tap into primal desires. Because BDSM is by nature about exploring sexual fantasies in a consensual way, it's no surprise that many folks want to find out what breaking free of our human shackles might feel like. Animal play, or pet play, is an apt avenue for bringing out the beast within.

In the 1980s and '90s, puppy play became increasingly popular—at least for gay men in the leather community. It usually involves dressing up like a dog or puppy and sharing a master-pet (or master-pup) dynamic with another person. As enthusiast Matt Baume explains in a piece for *The Stranger*:

> *If you're having trouble understanding the appeal of puppy play, just imagine how amazing it would be if there were a form of group relaxation where you could empty your mind of all your cares, forget all of your responsibilities, lower all of your defenses, and bypass small talk forever. Now imagine that vigorous cuddling and praise are key components of this relaxation technique. And did I mention snacks? You get snacks. Awesome.*

In the twenty-first century, puppy play is now an integral part of fetish gatherings both in private clubs and in public events, like San Francisco's Folsom Street Fair. It also shares aspects of pony play, which was documented as early as the 1950s in Irving Klaw fetish films like *Riding the Human Pony Girl*. Even your basic costumed role-play—what vanilla folks call Halloween—remains dominated by pet play outfits, including the ubiquitous "sexy kitty" for women that continues to be worn year after lipstick-nose, pointy-ear-headband, stuffed-tail-pinned-to-a-fishnet-ass year.

Really, embodying sexual abandon through cat aesthetics or role-play is just a husky purr and a playful paw away for anyone who wants to join in the fun. But why is it that cats bring out the kink in us? Cats may be sluts, but why are they kinky? For starters, it might be because early BDSM literature harnesses cat language and imagery as an intimate part of the interplay between dominance and submission, pleasure and pain.

BDSM, which stands alternately for bondage, domination/discipline, sadism/submission, and masochism, is an umbrella term for an array of erotic expressions. Although the acronym only dates back to the 1990s, the practice itself is far older—and remains stigmatized to this day. Contemporary kink communities are almost universally adamant about consent and conscious engagement with any BDSM practices, but it wasn't always this way.

In 1886, a German psychiatrist named Richard von Krafft-Ebing published *Psychopathia Sexualis*, a book which explored sexual deviancy and introduced terms like "sadism" and "masochism" into the English language along the way. "Sadism" was based upon the brutal domination that characterized sex in the Marquis de Sade's works, and "masochism" was based upon Leopold von Sacher-Masoch's characterization of the submissive relationship highlighted in *Venus in Furs*.

Cats and cat references can be found in both authors' writings.

For sadism's scatologically inclined forebearer, cats are wildly sexual women just waiting to be tamed. In his short story "Philosophy in the Bedroom," a dominant woman is referred to as a "wildcat" as she is instructed by the main (male) character to perform oral sex on another, younger woman. There is also the repeated appearance of the cat-o'-nine-tails* when Sade's characters deign to inflict delicious pain on their submissives, and Sade's use of a feline adjective as a term of endearment for his (quite literal) partner in crime. Over the years, Sade's wife, Renée-Pélagie Cordier de Montreuil, curated underage victims for his bloodiest orgies, and he, ever the charmer, called her his "celestial kitten."

In Leopold von Sacher-Masoch's crushing ode to submission *Venus in Furs*, cats take a far more mythical role. The protagonist's stunning, dominant muse Wanda wraps herself in the pelts of animals and embodies feline grace. The reader first sees her immortalized in a painting, "naked in a dark fur" on a sofa, "her right hand playing with a whip, her bare foot casually propped up a man, who lay before her like a slave, like a dog." From the moment she and Severin meet, Wanda is the cat to his canine. When Wanda's beloved slave asks her about her fondness for fur, she states that "the presence of cats exercises such a magic influence" on intelligent men.

"This is why these long-tailed Graces of the animal kingdom, these adorable, scintillating electric batteries have been the favorite animal of Mahommed, Cardinal Richelieu, Crebillon, Rousseau, Wieland," Wanda explains. "A woman wearing furs . . . is nothing else than a large cat, an augmented electric battery."

---

* The cat-o'-nine-tails, a whip consisting of nine knotted lengths of cotton cord that can lacerate skin on impact, was a commonly used weapon in Britain by the late 1600s. As it was kept in a bag until use, we're left with the phrase "let the cat out of the bag," which is a bit more brutal than the saying might seem.

Cats have never truly been domesticated as dogs have, so humans can never be a cat's true master. Much as they'll let us luxuriate in their soft folds, cats are their own keepers, most often keeping their humans on their toes, so it's an easy parallel to make between cats and a dominant/submissive relationship.

"If only she would use the whip again," muses Severin in *Venus in Furs*. "There is something uncanny in the kindness with which she treats me. I seem like a little captive mouse with which a beautiful cat prettily plays. She is ready at any moment to tear it to pieces, and my heart of a mouse threatens to burst."

Cats, in addition to having no gods and no masters, have a predilection for playing with their prey. Granted, it's nonconsensual and to the death, but this behavior makes it easy for cats to become the aspirational grande dame of dommes—a femme so in control of those in her service she could snuff them out at any moment if she chose to.

Instead, she forces them to enjoy their exquisite suffering for a few minutes more.

Animal behaviorists have different theories as to why cats might play with their prey. Some say it's to save energy and tire their tiny rodent, reptile, or insect victims out before delivering the kill shot. If kittens are nearby, it could be an opportunity for a hunting lesson. Another option is so-called "overflow play," which is to release pent up energy post-hunt. If a cat isn't used to having a smorgasbord of victims, it might want to prolong the fun. The capture and release and breathtaking, *s l o w* torture that cats engage in as predators are indeed reminiscent of the kind of play that kinky folks live for (albeit consensually).

It's difficult to assign any kind of will or desire beyond instinct to cats, but it's clear that in human terms, cats are more than "peculiarly lecherous," as Aristotle would have it. Instead, they have, in a sense, developed their own kind of BDSM. Cats were "kinky" long before the first Neanderthal decided to sexually repurpose a vine for a good time, before the Marquis de Sade conjured up abusive fantasies while locked away in the Bastille, and before Leopold von Sacher-Masoch lived the life of a lowly sub.

"Into Bondage?" asks the title of a recent article in *The Independent*, "It could be because of your cat, study finds." Not only do cats crack the whip in classic BDSM literature, but the parasite found in cats, *Toxoplasma gondii*, has also been linked to a sexual attraction to fear, danger, pain, and submissiveness in humans—all characteristics that are right at home in the kink community.

The 2016 study in question, authored by Jaroslav Flegr and Radim Kuba, analyzed data from 36,564 Czech and Slovak subjects, 5,087 of whom were free of toxoplasma infection and 741 who were infected. The researchers aimed to see if "infected and noninfected subjects differ in their sexual behavior, fantasies, and preferences when age, health, and the size of the place where they spent childhood were controlled." Using electronic surveys about human sexuality, Flegr and Radim were able to tease out that *T. gondii* does indeed correlate with one's sexual interests, but not quite in the ways you'd think. Their findings, published in the journal *Evolutionary Psychology*, show that those with toxoplasmosis might be turned on by kink, but that doesn't mean they actually go through with eschewing a vanilla lifestyle.

"Generally, infected subjects expressed higher attraction to nonconventional sexual practices, especially the BDSM-related practices," the authors write, "but they also reported to perform such activities less often than the toxoplasma-free subjects." The desire was there, but the flesh wasn't as willing as it was for folks whose behavior was unaffected by the parasite. As neat and tidy as the headlines like to make it sound, toxoplasmosis doesn't explain away the "crazy cat lady" stereotype, and it certainly doesn't account for the widespread interest in BDSM practices around the world.

To find out why people might not only be into kink but into animal play, I spoke with BDSM educator and creator of the *Why Are People into That?!* podcast, Tina Horn.

"Pet play or animal play is about invoking animal archetypes in your sexual expression or sexual relationships," Horn tells me. She differentiates between two distinct types of pet play: one that's part of a dynamic in a scene you engage in once or many times and another that's an ongoing animal identity. Either one brushes up against a variety of taboos, from bestiality to plain old sexual fantasy.

"There's something taboo about acknowledging the sexuality of animals and invoking the sexuality of animals," Horn says. "Role-play is taboo; it's considered freaky to pretend to be something that you're not sexually, which just doesn't make any sense. That's the best part about sex!" she exclaims. "I can only assume that's taboo because it gives people the opportunity to use their imaginations and that's dangerous, like for a woman to say, 'I am not what you tell me I am.'"

The ability to shift shape during sex is what makes pet play so appealing. It can allow those who indulge to tap into different gender expressions from their own or explore their own identity more deeply. It doesn't hurt that animals already come with gendered stereotypes, from cats (feminine) and dogs (masculine) to ponies (feminine) and pigs (masculine). "Obviously all animals are all genders," Horn says, but nevertheless, many animals are coded along the binary.

"For example, with cats, I could totally see a very masculine person having a kitty cat persona that might be more evocative of a feminine cat side," Horn poses. "Where being able to be a cat could help a very masculine person access a side of them that's seductive, that's coy and withholding, the side of them that's scratchy instead of punchy, the side of them that's slinky or sleek." And that's just what Dia Dynasty, a dominatrix who cofounded New York City dungeon La Maison du Rouge, offered one of her clients recently.

As someone who self-identifies as having both feline and serpentine energy, Dynasty has also incorporated cat play into her sessions with a male client. "One time I bought a cat mask on a whim from a Halloween store and brought it into one of my sessions," she explains. After telling her client that he was going to put it on, she laid an empty box on the floor and asked him, "What do cats do?" He immediately got into character, she says, "pawed at it for a moment, then he walked in a circle around it, spiraled into it, and then sat in it. I was so filled with glee!" she whispers. Enamored with the scene, Dynasty outfitted him with a bell collar for future sessions so she could always hear him coming.

This type of exploration can be freeing for a masculine person trying to explore femininity, but as Horn lays out, "a woman or femme person might also have a cat persona that helps them to more deeply sink into their femme side." In many cases, it's the gender play or behavioral modification that's at the heart of the animal play, not some spiritual connection to the animal in question.

"I am not a cat person," Horn reveals, "and am in fact allergic to cats and find them pretty unpleasant, but I sometimes find myself mewing and purring and pressing my head against my partner when I want a certain kind of attention," she says. "This was not something I decided to do; it kinda came out of me one day and I liked the result. Most days I'm more growly like a dog or bear and have a lot of other shifting creature personas, but sometimes I wanna be a sleek cat or cute kitten. I think this is a really good example of how it's the cat *persona* or cat *essence* that I'm tapping into, and seeking to be regarded as by my partner, rather than an aesthetic fetish or deep identification with the actual animal."

There are innumerable ways to channel animal energy, even for those who do not covet the animal in question. Shape-shifting through role-play can be done through costume, through behavior, through energetic frequency, and many shape-shifters cross the boundaries between animal and human with some kind of regularity. Selina Kyle isn't Catwoman when she goes to sleep. The *gnaghe* weren't able to live their lives in feminine aesthetics outside of Carnival season. However, there are the rare few who make a permanent transformation, channeling cat energy full-time. They aren't fictional characters from a David Bowie music video[†] or colorful pages from a comic book, but real women and femmes who live in a purrfect world of their own creation.

"I paint cats. I paint powerful women as cats," Isibella tells me, sweeping the champagne flute in her hand around the room, her gold, filigreed cat ears catching the light. Paintings of Madame de Pompadour, Marie Antoinette, Queen Victoria, and an unnamed courtesan as regal felines in voluminous gowns lean on side tables and on top of a vintage piano. There is a pot of Earl Grey brewing on the table in front of me and a tower of tea cookies. Baroque music plays softly as I sit on a velvet fainting sofa next to the proprietress of The Chateau, also known as Cat Girl Manor. Four slightly deflated balloons that spell out M E O W float behind us, the remains of a past celebration.

[†]   Not only did David Bowie write the title track for Paul Schrader's 1982 werecat film *Cat People*, but he also requested that a woman have a cat tail in the 2016 music video for "Blackstar," because, as he told director Johan Renck, "it's kind of sexual."

The heart of the Kittenplay community lies in a teal and pastel blue Victorian mansion in a rustic suburb of Colorado Springs. Like puppy play, pony play, and any kind of pet play, Kittenplay is a type of BDSM role-play, though some self-identified Kittens adhere to the aesthetic and lifestyle without the kink. Isibella, the founder of The Chateau, and a variety of Kittens live and work and play here, and dozens more attend gatherings, shows, and classes on various evenings. Ranches and dirt roads may pepper the surrounding countryside flanked by not-too-distant mountains, but within The Chateau time isn't linear, species morph and mingle, and sexual and intellectual freedom abounds.

"We talk about what makes a cat . . . they are very sensual creatures," Isibella muses. "The cat slinks up to you and rubs itself against you, the cat is purring, cats are very inherently in their nature sensual, they're sleek. When women embody or adopt that, they're channeling it," she explains. "That's different than cosplay or dressing up as a Kitten. They're actually two different things, and that doesn't mean you can't interlink the two. But there are a lot of women I think that channel feline energy without having to do that or need to do it: the visual versus channeling the spirit."

Inspired by her own kink inclinations and a deep connection with feline energy, Isibella, a UK-born and -bred event promoter and Egyptologist, named and midwifed this diverse group into existence over a decade ago.

"When I was younger, Kittenplay as a word didn't even exist," she says. "I remember thinking should I call this kitty play? Do I call this cat play? I was debating what word to use."

After Isibella's inaugural Kittenplay.net website garnered over 6,000 members, she knew her passions and predilections were shared around the world. In the ensuing years, Isibella has created YouTube tutorials and behind-the-scenes videos about her lifestyle and curated events around North America (Burning Man in Nevada, Vampire Balls in New Orleans, parties at Montreal Fetish Weekend). At present, she and her fellow Kittens appear in magazines, documentaries, and TV shows, and the #kittenplay hashtag on Instagram boasts over a million posts that feature women and feminine folks wearing ears and tails and lingerie and playful feline getups.

"You don't need to be wearing cat ears to channel feline qualities, but as part of the persona the visual is important." Isibella gestures to the pair she wears that have been handcrafted in Venice. "I've worn them so much recently, when I don't wear them it's like an extension of myself is missing." Today, she isn't wearing a tail.

Just as there are Maine Coons, Russian Blues, Bombays, tabbies, and Bengals, there are different breeds of human Kittens, too. These include (but are certainly not limited to) Domesticated Kittens, Feral Kittens, Vampurrs, and Nekos; the last are often in it for the cosplay, a Japanese/English portmanteau of "costume play" with roots in sci-fi and comics convention culture.

A self-identified "Domesticated Kitten" and submissive who is collared by a dominant partner, Isibella tells me she'd be a fluffy Persian in feline form. "I couldn't go outside into the world because I'd die very quickly," she chuckles. "I'm refined. I like opera. I drink champagne. However, my best friend, Jenny, is a Feral Kitten. She is a car mechanic for a living; she's also a Chateau model. She's very alternative. She'll never be owned by anyone," Isibella says. "She still has a collar, but it's a collar she collared herself. She owns herself."

For those unfamiliar with the practice, collaring is an act between a dominant and submissive or master and slave. This consensual dynamic can be explored both inside and outside the bedroom, and as many in the community know, it is the slave or submissive who often, ironically, can call the shots. Still, not all Kittens are kinky, Isibella affirms, even though that's her orientation.

"I'd definitely like to make sure some people are aware that there are those who just want to dress up and cosplay as Kittens," Isibella says. "They don't want to bring fetish into it. That's their lifestyle choice, and it's perfectly OK. I never try to thrust fetish upon everyone. It's definitely my personal choice and part of my dynamic, but that doesn't mean it's everyone's dynamic."

After taking in my aura and outfit, which included fishnets, cowboy boots with cobweb stitching, and a spandex dress covered in spiders, the proprietress of The Chateau decides I am a "Vampurr," one of the newer types of Kitten—a vampire/goth/Kitten hybrid. She mentions that they're just about to begin decorating for Halloween, and my thoughts turn to the occult. I ask if most Kittens practice magic, and she says she'd love if that were the case, but they are only starting to catch up with her interests.

Identifying as a left-hand path practitioner, Isibella has long been a student of the occult and now hosts monthly "Esoteric Evenings" in the basement of The Chateau to share her knowledge with other Kittens. Sigil making, meditation, tarot, and manifestation are all part of what she hopes will empower those who attend.

As kink has been mainstreamed by *Fifty Shades of Grey* (for better or for worse), witchcraft, too, has been mainstreamed in the past five years with a surge in millennial popularity (for better or for worse). Still, there is stigma associated with the left-hand path, which, in Western occultism, has historical ties to so-called "black magic," Satanism, and sex magic. "Everyone's like, well, left-hand path is so evil," Isibella says, "but the left-hand path is more about survival, self-preservation. . . . For women, it's very difficult for us to put ourselves first; we're already at a disadvantage by just being born as a certain gender, even now," she says.

And where do cats all fit into this, I ask?

"In terms of the occult, you can't deny—especially when you talk about witchcraft—that cats are inherently a part of that, having familiars. Are cats and the occult inherently linked? Absolutely. Is it no mistake that then witches are these very feminine creatures which are persecuted for being too sexual and are then associated with cats? Absolutely." She then regales me with the story of *Carmilla*, the first vampire tale, predating Dracula, about a lesbian vampire who shape-shifts into a cat. Halfway through, her parrot and familiar Crowley, named after occultist Aleister Crowley, tries to drink champagne out of her glass and she swats him away. "He's still a baby," she smiles.

Without using political language, Isibella is nevertheless firm in her commitment to diversity within the community, noting that there are Kittens of all races, orientations, body types, and gender identities.

"I love that there is this variety," she continues, her blue eyes lighting up. "That's what makes the community fun. You just really want to make it as diverse as possible and welcoming for everyone to have an archetype."

She dips into her esoteric roots to elaborate and, in the process, encapsulates what is so appealing about being part of the Kitten-play community.

"You know you look at tarot cards and you've got the priest-ess, the empress, the queen, different archetypes? The idea is if you read them they fit a different type of feminine energy or persona. We look in our lives for archetypes. We do. All women do. We say, 'I like this and I'm going to shape my image around this because it feels comfortable and I want it to be an expression of who I am to the outside world as well.'"

For Isibella and the women and femmes at The Chateau—and the Kittenplay community at large—cats offer all the archetypal inspiration they need to transform into themselves.

Fresh off of my foray into Cat Girl Manor, my thoughts returned to another icon of cats and kink. Catwoman was the one who got me curious about BDSM in the first place, but her personal proclivities always seemed too diffuse to nail down. DC Comics designed her character with a sadistic streak from the get-go, but her nature is still unclear. Is Catwoman a dom? A sub? A (s)witch?

It depends on who's playing.

In the very first episode of *Batman* #1 published in 1943, Batman is all about his dominant daddy vibes. When he nabs the jewel thief known as The Cat, he tears off her disguise as she protests and squirms. "Quiet or papa spank!" he cautions, his hand hovering above her backside.

This power differential shifts when Batman proceeds to kneel at The Cat's feet, unwrapping a bandage around her ankle where she has hidden her spoils. He holds her foot in his hand with the grace of an appreciative fetishist. She quips, "What's the use. I know when I'm licked! Go ahead!" her choice of words not-so-subtly hinting at podophilia and oral sex.

Theirs is a tasty perversion of the Cinderella trope, the glass slipper a purloined necklace, and a man and a woman who pretend to be human bat and cat hybrids, almost living happily ever after.

From this first flirtatious encounter, both implicit and explicit BDSM practices are peppered throughout Catwoman's appearances in comics, television, and film. Selina Kyle's alter ego becomes known for topping from the bottom and only acquiesces to the Caped Crusader to trick him into thinking he has the upper hand.

She mostly controls the rules of engagement. There are plenty of close calls, but Catwoman always escapes to play another day.

Years later, after the comic censors had eased up and Catwoman took to the small screen, she was back on her game. The kinkily titled "Scat! Darn Catwoman" episode from 1967 is filled with BDSM gags. The show opens with Julie Newmar's Catwoman and her protégé, Pussycat, played by pop icon Lesley Gore, towering above Batman, who is tied up on the ground. Catwoman's lair is decked out with scarlet-flocked wallpaper, burning candelabras, and leopard-print tufted furniture—classic boudoir vibe. The ropes that crisscross Batman are a visual nod to bondage, and he squirms as his muscled chest tries to resist their torque. Catwoman and Pussycat delight in his suffering.

By the 1980s and '90s, Catwoman's sex life becomes more fleshed out. In Frank Miller's *Batman: Year One* published in 1987 and Mindy Newell's *Catwoman* mini-series published in 1989, Selina Kyle's backstory is entirely updated. No longer a victim of amnesia, she's a sex worker whose pimp gives her a cat costume to wear with clients. She's also been gifted a whip that she later learns to use with the help of a grizzled combat instructor.

In *Batman Returns*, Catwoman's kink factor is amplified with a latex costume (designed by Mary Vogt and Bob Ringwood) that is slathered in silicone for structural purposes. With just the right lighting, it makes her character literally drip with danger as she goes head-to-head with Batman.

Celebrating Batman and Catwoman's exploits in Tim Burton's film, Emily Asher-Perrin et al. composed an homage to Gotham's kink in a *Tor.com* article titled "We Need a Kink in Our Stories: BDSM Characters in Your Favorite Genre Fiction." The authors argue that Batman and Catwoman's fighting back and forth never boils over into one party fully dominating the other, but instead it is a never-ending game of cat and mouse that's charged with every sharp-tongued riposte.

"The fight at first seems to be functioning as foreplay," the authors write, "but gradually it becomes clear that this is the main event. This is how they communicate, and how they express their complicated love and admiration for each other. In *Batman Returns*, we get an enthusiastic, consensual, totally equal BDSM relationship that puts *Secretary* to shame."

To be fair, we are never privy to Batman and Catwoman or Bruce Wayne and Selina Kyle entering into any kind of official BDSM contract or even discussing their kinks with one another, which is a vital part of any consensual sexual practice. For fantasy's sake, because this is indeed many a person's fantasy, it's nice to imagine they do, given how much the two seem to enjoy their libidinal encounters.

A decade later, the bat and the cat are still at it in the 2004 Catwoman comic "Date Knight" by Darwyn Cooke. As the Caped Crusader and Catwoman fight across town, she leads the charge, finally besting Batman as the city lies in smoking ruins behind them. The scene ends with him hanging upside down by a rope she has rigged. "If you play your cards right, maybe you can take me out again next Saturday," she purrs, covering his face with red-lipsticked kisses.

The most unambiguous interaction between Gotham City's finest occurs in *Catwoman Volume 1: The Game*; however, it doesn't rely on innuendo—or a relationship between Bruce Wayne and Selina Kyle—to show us the full extent of Batman and Catwoman's sexual appetites.

Within the first few pages of Judd Winick and Guillem March's 2012 collaboration, Catwoman is seducing Batman, again, as they throw their bodies around the room. "Most of the costumes stay on," Catwoman says, "I'm not trying to be crude, but it plays out mostly like a bar fight. Bodies get hurled around. Things get broken. Some pretty filthy language is uttered . . . And tomorrow, there's definitely going to be some bruising."

Their rough sex role-play ends with perhaps the most intimate moment of all, as Batman, still masked, his arm around a still-masked Catwoman, asks her if she's OK after their session. She melts into his embrace for a moment and nods. It is the closest we've come to a realistic depiction of consent and pleasure in a BDSM relationship.

Cats may be sluts, but they need aftercare, too.

Hex-Ray Vision and the Feline Gaze

Crescent moons bloom into black saucers. Third eyelids spring open and closed. Watching with cool clarity, their aperture eyes expand and contract with the light. They sense and stare, as focus is fixated with laser precision, prey or playmate in view.

Whether you awake in the morning to a tiny tiger staring love daggers at you or open the door to a shock of two glowing orbs in the dark, being looked at by a cat—really looked at—is an arresting experience. The feline gaze is singular, savage, spellbinding.

With night vision that is at least six times better than humans', a cat's iridescent eyes take in 50 percent more light than our own. The reflective retinal structure in feline eyes, the *tapetum lucidum*, amplifies available light so they can better see in the dark. Cats even have a third eyelid, the *palpebra tertia*, to protect their remarkable peepers. Although we'll never know with certainty what they see, a cat's detached, penetrating gaze can be the stuff of daydreams and nightmares. Unblinking and unknowable, it can be just as sinister as it is seductive.

Between humans, a glance can signal the difference between a threat and a joke, a come-on and a casual comment. Looking and being looked at are a central part of how we communicate, of power dynamics, of sex, which is why gender theorists are so preoccupied with the act of looking and *the gaze*.

Whether scrolling through Instagram or beholding the sculpted curves of the Venus of Willendorf, looking at female bodies is a cultural ritual unto itself. Although the male gaze may be the dominant one that structures how women and feminine folks are viewed by the world—and often how they view themselves—that doesn't mean it is the only gaze of import. French philosopher Jacques Derrida discovered this jarring fact one morning when he was confronted, naked, by the gaze of his female cat.

Something so mundane might have slipped past a less perceptive man, but Derrida was nothing if not exceedingly observant. He noticed he felt ashamed as his cat looked at him in the buff, undressing his very being with her penetrating eyes. He wondered if others had experienced this confrontation between animal and human in such a way that paradoxically affirmed their fundamental differences *and* their sameness. So, being a post-structuralist of import, he sat down and wrote a ten-hour lecture about it.

The published translation of the lecture, "The Animal That Therefore I Am (More to Follow)," describes the encounter with his pet as "the single, incomparable and original experience of the impropriety that would come from appearing in truth naked, in front of the insistent gaze of the animal, a benevolent or pitiless gaze, surprised or cognizant." Derrida likens the cat's gaze to that of "a seer, a visionary or extra-lucid blind one" and affirms the "immense symbolic responsibility with which our culture has always charged the feline race." This laborious preamble is really just to say: Derrida really liked cats.

But why was his encounter so unique? Derrida explains that it was because few philosophers have ever considered an animal's point of view. Despite thousands of years of coexisting with cats and other animals, no notable thinker has discussed the act of being "*seen*" by an animal. Sure, they theorized about animals in an abstract way, but philosophers in a lineage from Descartes and Kant to Heidegger and Lacan have ignored animal subjectivity altogether.

"It is as if the men representing this configuration had seen without being seen," Derrida muses, "seen the animal without being seen by it; without being seen naked by someone who, from deep within a life called animal, and not only by means of the gaze, would have obliged them to recognize, at the moment of address, that this was their affair, their lookout."

Is it any wonder these same men failed to seriously consider female subjectivity?

There is a compelling parallel between the way men have historically used, regulated, and ascribed behaviors and idiosyncrasies to the bodies of animals and the bodies of women. The two have been consistently compared and conflated—all instinct and no intellect—and deemed wild enough to be desirable yet ultimately unimportant—disposable even.

Without having to know much about post-structuralist theory, there is a lot of what Derrida writes that is quite intuitive. Any pet owner with a pulse can stare into their cat's eyes and hopefully see that there is more than just an unthinking, unfeeling corpus of fur and bone staring back. And, by extension, one hopes anyone can stare into a woman's eyes, too, and see her humanity—although neither are guaranteed.

The gravitas of the gaze is not to be underestimated, whether feline or female. Throughout history, both have been marginalized and mythologized. Cats' eyes and women's eyes have been the supposed cause of malice or magic, depending on who's in charge of writing said history.

In ancient China, the goddess Li Shou appeared in the form of a cat, lived a life of sybaritic leisure, and kept the order of the world in check. She controlled the sun with her pupils, so peering into the eyes of a cat was said to be the best way to tell time.

In ancient Greece, the philosopher Plutarch attributed a synergistic relationship between cat's eyes and the moon, noting that their pupils would wax and wane with its "heavenly body."

In ancient Egypt, the cat goddess Bast was also associated with the sun. As protectress of the pharaoh, she was often depicted as a cat-headed woman and the embodiment of the eye of the sun god Ra. The eye of Ra was an extension of his powers and a violent force used to defeat all enemies of Egypt. In the glowing orbs of a cat's eyes, Egyptians saw the eternal flames of their sun deity. Like Ra, even in the darkness, a cat can shine a light.

Similarly, the snake-tressed Greek gorgon Medusa used her mighty eyes to vanquish her enemies by turning them all to stone. Incensed at her ability to make men hard as a rock, the "hero" Perseus slayed Medusa and kept her head to wield as a weapon.

Witches, too, were believed to harness the power of a malicious glance—sometimes called the "evil eye"—in early modern Europe. Countless writings of the time from court records to witch-hunting manuals warn of a witch's wicked glare. There was no shortage of afflicted folks bemoaning their neighborhood hag's hex-ray vision. A 1646 treatise about witches by John Gaule says that witches could enact their curses through a "glare, or squint, or peep at with an envious and evil eye."

One 1690 text cited by Lizanne Henderson in *Witchcraft and Folk Belief in the Age of Enlightenment: Scotland, 1670–1740* documents a Scottish belief that witches' eyes weren't reflective like standard-issue mortal eyes and could kill on command. In *The Discoverie of Witchcraft*, Reginald Scot says that women in the Eastern European region of Scythia had "inchanting or bewitching eies."

Across Europe, witches were reported making children sick and causing animals to die with their "ill eyes." In America, during the Salem witch trials, Mary Osgood was accused of bewitching two other women "by the glance of her eyes," and Abigail Faulkner was purported to use the "evil eye" on some of the town girls who devolved into "grievious fitts" when she entered the courtroom.

"In witchcraft cases, the evil eye was a form of maleficium, arguably the purest form of maleficium because it operated solely by the witch's malice rather than the properties of herbs, ointments, potions or charms," writes historian William E. Burns in *Witch Hunts in Europe and America*. To make matters more complicated, witches were also thought to influence those presiding over their trials with the power of the evil eye.

Because of the close ties between witches and cats, felines were believed to have the power of the evil eye as well. Catching even a hint of a vertical pupil in passing could be dangerous.

Sorcerer-cum-Christian St. Cyprian of Antioch said it was possible to conjure a diminutive devil through the eyes of a black cat. Physician Ambroise Paré explained in his sixteenth-century treatise *Of Poisons* that the stare of a cat could cause a vulnerable victim to lose consciousness. Even Shakespeare mentions the ominous "cat with eyne of burning coal" in his 1619 play *Pericles*.

The Talmud ascribes second sight to cats. It can be passed on to humans by pulverizing the placenta of a firstborn black female cat, setting it ablaze, and making a powder of the remains. If you put this powder in your eyes, you, too, will see the demons around you.

But though cats may have had the power of the evil eye in many belief systems, their entire being was believed by others to be powerful enough to occlude human vision entirely. Both European ceremonial magic and American hoodoo practices have been using black cat body parts in invisibility spells for centuries.

Albertus Magnus, mentor to Saint Thomas Aquinas, believed that invisibility was at your fingertips if you wore on your thumb the ear of a black cat boiled in the milk of a black cow.

A common hoodoo invisibility spell noted by author and folklorist Zora Neale Hurston involved boiling a black cat alive and finding your way to the one bone that will grant you the ability to disappear. Then, you must slip it into your mouth to start the spell.

"If you get the black cat's bone," she writes in "Hoodoo in America," "you can travel out of the sight of people and do whatever you want to do. But to get it, you must sell yourself to the devil."

In ancient Arab belief, the cat's-eye stone, chrysoberyl, was used to produce invisibility in battle.

Viewed as pets, as kept creatures, as a feast for the eyes, women and cats have historically been treated like "something seen and not seeing," to expand upon Derrida's assertion. Because of this, the feline and the feminine have been alternately idolized and demonized. The impact of their unfettered glances has reverberated around the world.

In his lecture about the gaze of his little cat, it's notable that Derrida emphasizes how male philosophers have been the culprits in denying animals their subjectivity—"males and not females, for that difference is not insignificant here" he writes—but the philosopher is not quite a feminist hero. As cultural theorist and cyber-feminist Donna Haraway explains, Derrida becomes so caught up in his own shame at the gaze of his cat that he forgets about her perspective by the end of his lecture.

"But with his cat, Derrida failed a simple obligation of companion species; he did not become curious about what the cat might actually be doing, feeling, thinking, or perhaps making available to him in looking back at him that morning," she writes in *When Species Meet*. "He missed a possible invitation, a possible introduction to other-worlding."

It is this other-worlding that is made possible by opening yourself up to an animal's perspective. Occultists and magical practitioners have found ineffable synergy in feline eye contact for centuries, and it has thus become a potent force in ritual and spellcraft. Scientists, too, have found verifiable power in the feline gaze.

To meet the prolonged gaze of another person can cause the release of the bonding hormone oxytocin in the human brain, flooding your system with feelings that often translate to connectedness and warmth. This is the case when we look at and touch our partners but also when we look at and touch our pets. It doesn't matter the species with whom we share a glance: humans get a sustaining jolt from being seen.

When we talk about being seen in popular slang these days, it doesn't just mean your visage passes through someone else's line of sight. It means to be enveloped in acceptance. It means to be understood by another beyond the visual and into the metaphysical. It is honest, holistic. What would it mean to look with as much intensity as you are looked at, to have your gaze upended and returned?

To be really seen? The potency of the feline and female gaze has long been scrutinized and mythologized, but most of all it has been overlooked—or, perhaps more accurately, underlooked.

Art Cats—Sex and the Sphinx

The cat is my medium.
–Carolee Schneemann

There are hundreds of cats in the Metropolitan Museum of Art. Some have crept across canvases; others have clawed their way out of ivory or wood. Still others sit atop decadent baubles and amulets or are frozen in time as bronze silhouettes. These cats who make the Beaux-Arts palace their forever home emigrated across continents, sometimes solo, but often with a female companion. Immortalized together, they present in parallel poses, their flesh in slinky symmetry.

Two great bronze lions pull Roman mother goddess Cybele in a statuette from the second century AD. All three have erect postures—proud—exuding sovereign grace.

The unholy sabbath depicted in Hans Baldung Grien's 1510 chiaroscuro woodcut *The Witches* features a nude witch and cat, back to back, their voluptuous folds a mirror image in the midst of some kind of conjuring.

Kitagawa Utamaro's woodblock print *A woman with a cat* from 1793 centers on a beautiful maiden in translucent gossamer silk. She sits in front of a needlework box, holding a piece of fabric in her teeth as the cat playing at her feet does the same. Her bare breasts are illuminated through her kimono. She and her feline counterpart are content in their mimetic modes of sensual play.

Jan Cornelisz Vermeyen's *Girl with a Cat* etching from 1545 depicts a subject in a traditional white Dutch head covering and a solemn countenance, staring ahead, eyes downcast. The cat in her arms mirrors the pathos and direction of her glance.

Sometimes the cat isn't merely a woman's double, though, but the two are in the process of becoming one. Marc Chagall's *Cat Metamorphosized into a Woman*, a 1927 etching, highlights a woman mid-shape-shift. Her elbow is propped up against a table as her oval skull becomes triangular, nose narrowing into a snout.

In similar fashion, Wanda Wulz's *Io + gatto* gelatin silver print of 1932 features the artist's severe face overlaid with the black and white feline markings of her cat, whiskers unfurled across the edges of her cropped bob, one pupil a vertical slit, another an obsidian orb.

Cat symbology in art of the past millennium is strikingly consistent. Cats are sensual, cats are demonic, cats are feminine. Cats are a reflection of women, or least reveal how men perceive women to be. There is a striking difference in depictions of cats and women, however, when feline and feminine forms are captured not only by women, but by women who love cats. And few artists have exemplified the feral feminine like Leonor Fini and Carolee Schneemann.

Fini was well-versed in the modalities of shape-shifting. The Argentinian-born and Italian-bred Surrealist painter and iconoclast favored sphinxes, witches, monstrous feminine hybrids, and androgynous bodies in her work. She was an avid fan of masquerades and continually changed her appearance by dyeing her hair kaleido-scopic colors and wearing extravagant costumes to fancy balls and everyday affairs. She kept multiple lovers of all genders and shared her bed with many Persian cats. Fini was also the first woman to turn the tables and paint an erotic male nude. Her fascination with metamorphosis is reflected most vividly, however, in paintings of sphinxes with flowing hair and feminine faces, which are sometimes depictions of the artist herself.

In myth, the riddling Greek sphinx has been relegated to the monstrous feminine category. When the "hero" Odysseus solved her riddle, she took her own life in defeat. But what do we really know about the sphinx besides her monstrosity? Film theorist Teresa de Lauretis points out in *Alice Doesn't: Feminism, Semiotics, Cinema* that "the Sphinx, like the other ancient monsters, [has] survived inscribed in hero narratives, in someone else's story, not [her] own." The author argues that the sphinx's power, like Medusa's, has been expressed in the "luring of man's gaze into the 'dark continent,' as Freud put it, the enigma of femininity."

Fini's sphinxes, however, challenge this male/female, monster/hero duality.

In *The Shepherdess of the Sphinxes* painted in 1941, Fini unveils a human woman with a shepherd's crook watching over a field of bare-breasted sphinxes. They sit gamely: paws out, tails curled, haunches round, beckoning with otherworldly booty. There are cracked, empty eggshells, bones, and flowers strewn across the arid landscape. Some look wistful, some watchful, some seductive.

Art historian and Fini specialist Rachael Grew notes that the way the human woman "straddles her shepherd's crook is highly suggestive, creating a connection not only to the witch's broom . . . but also to sexual autonomy." The sphinxes are sexually autonomous in their own right, too. With nary a man in sight, they are positioned not only as destroyers but creatrices—as evidenced by the many hatched eggs.

"Fini's sphinxes can also be equated with the Great Mother goddess and parthenogenesis," Grew explains in "Sphinxes, witches and little girls: reconsidering the female monster in the art of Leonor Fini." Like the female artists who create without the input of their male peers, Grew suggests that so, too, can these sphinxes procreate on their own, just as some ancient goddesses were wont to do.

In Fini's oeuvre, the divine feminine and demonic feminine share equal billing. She is as much interested in benevolent mother goddesses as she is deviant witches, and cats are crucial to both. Her paintings and drawings of women, cats, and witches play into stereotypes about women just as much as they demolish them. Fini painted cats alone (horned ones, winged ones); women and cats (playing, cuddling, holding court); and witches and cats (haunting, stalking, riding on broomsticks in parallel motion). Fini conjured the feline and the feminine in a variety of magical and mundane circumstances, but it is *La Vie Ideale* (The Ideal Life) from 1950 that positions her as the first cat lady of art.

The self-portrait of sorts features the artist in the center, her black hair cascading, the folds of her gown slipping languidly off her shoulders, her legs open, elbow resting on one knee in a confident womanspread—a feline pose if there ever was one. Six cats prowl and sleep and play beneath her feet: some domesticated, some wild. The circular backdrop behind her is a kind of tattered, black halo. It's a scene fit for a "queen of the underworld," as she called herself, complete with feline emissaries and allies who heighten her magic.

Like Fini, multidisciplinary American artist Carolee Schneemann infused the feline and the feminine in confrontational, sex-positive work long before the sex-positive movement even had a name. The two may have featured their beloved cats in entirely different ways but were equally inspired by their physicality, sensuality, and mystery.

One of Schneemann's earliest films from 1965, *Fuses*, shows the artist having sex with a male partner as her cat Kitch curiously looks on. Schneemann manipulated the film itself by burning, staining, and drawing on it while simultaneously reframing how female sexuality can appear in fine art and pornography.

"I wanted to put into that materiality of film the energies of the body, so that the film itself dissolves and recombines and is transparent and dense," Schneemann explains in *The Tactile Eye: Touch and the Cinematic Experience.* "It is different from any pornographic work that you've ever seen—that's why people are still looking at it! And there's no objectification or fetishization of the woman."

This bold film defies the passivity inherent in many depictions of the female sexual experience, and it's no coincidence that a cat is part of the scene. Kitsch plays a supporting role but also serves as a signifier of femininity and of feral appetites. *Fuses* and Schneemann's other work would go on to become foundational to the burgeoning movement of feminist art, and her cats would continue to be her artistic subjects (so much so that the Museum of the Moving Image devoted a whole day to them in 2016 christened "Mysteries of the Pussies: The Cat Films of Carolee Schneemann").

By the 1980s, Schneemann had begun a project that would focus with explicit precision upon the romance between women and their cats. Each day, she documented her morning ritual of being awakened from a slumber—*Sleeping Beauty*-style—with a deep, openmouthed kiss by her cat, Cluny. Keeping a camera next to her bed, Schneemann captured these exchanges between 1981 and 1988.

As she told Priscilla Frank at the *Huffington Post*, "I didn't invite it but didn't refuse. . . . He put his tongue in my mouth. It felt like a mystical lover from a lost time that had come back in the form of a cat." Schneemann did not orchestrate this interaction; her only choice in the matter was indulging the cat in this behavior and documenting it. She continued the project between 1990 and 1998 with another cat, Vesper, and combined photographs from both series into a 2008 film, *Infinity Kisses—The Movie*.

To some cat lovers who see no shame in swapping spit with their cat, Schneemann's work is relatable, charming, familiar. To others, it verges on bestiality.

Hyperallergic described Schneemann's cat photos as having "a deeply discomfiting eroticism to them, as well as a latent morbidity," because the artist is often lying on her back. One particularly memorable shot has a black and white paw stretch out against her neck, the way you might grasp your beloved as you go in for a kiss. There is one dominant species in the series, and it is not *Homo sapiens*. Schneemann's cats are always on top.

"*Infinity Kisses* landed with a silent thud in the art world, seemingly too eccentric and repulsive to warrant attention," writes Sasha Archibald in the Walker Art Center's magazine. "The piece proved an heir to the cautious repugnance relegated to cat women, those self-elected pariahs who have exchanged human company for feline and carry the molt to prove it."

Schneemann, no stranger to courting controversy, was aware of what she was doing by releasing the series into the world. "The intimacy between cat and woman becomes a refraction of the viewers' attitudes to self and nature, sexuality and control, the taboo and the sacred," the artist writes in *Imaging Her Erotics: Essays, Interviews, Projects*. The work speaks to the "dissolution of the boundaries between human and animal, reason and the irrational."

What makes both Schneemann's and Fini's work so compelling is that they are merely documenting their fantastical realities—and, arguably, the realities of many women who have been shunned and demonized for having what is deemed a *too close* relationship with their cats.

"I experience an erotic world where there is no divergence, no hostility, where everything mixes together," Fini once said. "I like to feel myself in a state of metamorphosis like certain animals and certain plants."

Ever the shape-shifters, Fini and Schneemann have literally drawn and redrawn the boundaries between woman and animal, feline and feminine. Through work that features cats and women in egalitarian modes of intimacy, both artists offer a vision of an idealized, electric subjectivity that transcends sex and species.

Feline Glamour (Magic)

A feast for the eyes, felines are fashion's eternal muse. Enviable coats, an evocative stare, sinewy grace on the ground, and a disposition for drama have made cats beloved by designers, stylists, and cat ladies alike. They inspire striking makeup and fabric patterns. Their elegant silhouettes and adorable mugs feature in countless designs. Few species have stalked the catwalks of couturiers, popped up in bargain basements, and adorned the backs of our ancestors like members of the Felidae family.

The crown jewel of feline fashion has historically been the cat print. Wearing the pelt patterns of wildcats signals strength and even an untamed streak. Tiger, leopard, jaguar, cheetah: these stripes and spots have become the mark of feral femininity.

As Jo Weldon explains in *Fierce: The History of Leopard Print*: "The desire to dress like a dangerous animal has a specific intention to it. . . . Those who chose to wear leopard print may not mean to say that they are predators, but they are definitely saying they are not prey."

Leopard print, though worn by men and masculine people, has become predominately associated with femininity—particularly in the West. Weldon cites disparate, boundary-breaking women and femmes who have all shared a preference for wearing leopard print, from sword-fighting champion Jaguarina and the first female cab-driver in New York City Wilma K. Russey to pinup legend Bettie Page, actress Dolores del Rio, singer and Catwoman star Eartha Kitt, drag legend Divine, and first ladies Jackie Kennedy and Michelle Obama. These brazen babes may not have much in common besides leopard print, but none could be accused of being meek.

Feline prints are just as much about attitude as they are aesthetics. The bold femininity they represent isn't likely to become outmoded. Leopard or tiger or cheetah prints may at times be trendy, but not a mere trend. *Elle* magazine affirmed that big-cat prints will "never go out of style" and are "forever chic." "They may be more popular one season than another," writes Harriet Stewart, "but, on the whole, they are forever pieces that form the cornerstones of our wardrobes."

Cat fashion is by no means limited to wildcat prints, though. Designers have been envisioning even more ways to incorporate cats into our wardrobes as of late. Streetzie's literal kitten heels feature a faux fur face—ears, whiskers, reflective eyes, and all—on the front of a flirty open-toed pump. Pop star Ariana Grande teamed up with Brookstone to create wireless Bluetooth headphones with cat ears on top that flash colorful lights and act as miniature speakers. And, for the fetishists, there are even butt plugs with plush cat tails attached to the opposite end for full feline play options.

As ever, cat-adjacent items run the gamut from coquettish to outright erotic. Wearing cat prints and cat accessories is a visible sign of heightened sexuality in untamed women that we've come to take for granted. The addition of actual cats only further elucidates the connection.

Cat's eye makeup, whether done with liquid liner or eye shadow (or both), is yet another way humans have tried to appropriate feline beauty for ourselves. *Teen Vogue* doubled down on the cat eye trend in a spread photographed by BriAnne Wills (author of the book *Girls and Their Cats*) titled "We Paired Fall's 6 Coolest Cat Eyes with Kittens, Because Obviously." The models sport various reimaginings of cat's eye makeup while rescue kittens serve face in each photo. The spread reflects a youthful sexuality, not full-on predatory, but not without bite. With so many options for changing your face into a feline visage, "you'll want to try them all right meow," writer Emily Gaynor quips.

This was hardly the inaugural fashion spread that cast cats to enhance a product's appeal. Dolce & Gabbana featured the grande dame of sex, Madonna, mid-stroke on a black-and-white kitty in one of its ads, and Lanvin offered two slinky black cats bookmarking a reclining model in another. Photographer Mario Testino created an iconic set of cat images in 2008 when he shot Claudia Schiffer for German *Vogue* with a stunning, po-faced Persian. In one photo, she reclines on a leather sofa holding the white, long-haired cat above her face. Her arches lift out of her spike heels, her white blouse sheer, her red lips parted. The cat's round countenance is calm in this suspended state. In another, she takes on the cat's role herself, wearing a black masquerade cat mask. The final and most evocative shot of Testino's has Schiffer wearing a garment of white taxidermied mice. The plush white cat is folded into her arms. Both feline and female project soul-penetrating stares. The name of the series was simply titled "Sex."

Designer Karl Lagerfeld's cat Choupette (aka "@chanelofficial and @fendi pussy" to whom he bequeathed part of his multimillion-dollar fortune upon his 2019 death) also appears in various sensually minded shoots. In a particularly racy spread from 2012 called "Glamour Puss," Laetitia Casta brandishes the Birman cat for *V Magazine*. The imagery brushes up against a kink aesthetic with lots of black and leather as Casta and the cat frolic together on a bed with the Eiffel Tower as a backdrop. Paris, cats, half-naked women: nothing could be more obvious when it comes to selling sex.

Cat fashion isn't always aligned with the conventionally attractive, though. In fact, it can also be the aesthetic opposite of seduction in a glossy magazine. One prevailing stereotype of cat *lady* fashion is anything but sexy, according to the masses. Think a frumpy woman of a certain age wearing fur-covered sweatpants and an oversized shirt with a cartoon kitty saying, "I Don't Do Mousework"—or something like that. You get where I'm going. There's nothing inherently wrong with this look, but it wasn't crafted to appeal to the male gaze, which is the defining rubric by which fashion and female attractiveness have historically been judged.

The feminine walk prized across continents is cat incarnate. Although the "catwalk" wouldn't be associated with fashion until 1942—it was a long, narrow runway on ships and in theaters before that—a cat's silent, supple pad has been part of the movement ideal held up for women. Like the fog, ladies are meant to come in on little cat feet—seen, yet stealthy; unheard.

Every gait has a story to tell. Class, culture, gender, emotion: they all play out beneath our feet. As the witch trials raged in the early modern era, urbanization caused its own shift in beliefs and behaviors. With more people living among strangers in closer and closer quarters, taking in the sights through a stroll allowed for new ways to interact with the city and break away from being stacked like sardines inside. Ever since, there's been no shortage of advice for women as they move about the world.

In 1558, Italian poet Giovanni della Casa revealed that the correct feminine way to walk would be to "go so softe and demurely, as a maide or a wife."

"Walk slowly, gracefully! . . . Erect, yet, at the same time, easy and elegant," implored Florence Hartley in *The Ladies' Book of Etiquette* published in 1860.

"Clench your bottom, tip your pelvis slightly up, and let your hips take you forward," instructs William Hanson, one of the UK's leading modern etiquette experts. "Push your weight through the pelvis. Your ankle gets lifted up, knee bent, and then straighten onto the floor. A traditional walk is heel-toe, and whilst in heels this is still true, it shouldn't be as pronounced as when in flat shoes." Hanson concludes: "Some find it helpful to picture a feline movement."

Body language transmits so much information about gender identity that those attempting to shape-shift theirs are often given feline directives. Drag foremother RuPaul Charles, who greets his contestants with a "Hey, kitty girl!" refrain, tells the drag queens on his long-running show, *RuPaul's Drag Race*, to "sissy that walk" (i.e., feminize it).

A music video for RuPaul's 2014 song "Sissy That Walk" based on the catchphrase offers plenty of feline examples to convey his instructions. Right off the bat, one of the first shots we're shown is a black panther sashaying down a runway illuminated in fuchsia light. RuPaul's black sequined legs soon follow. He's wearing a collar and a catsuit with sheer cutouts that look as if a pair of claws has slashed through it as he sings about his "pussy" and the panther's regal face flashes across the screen. Cats, it would seem, are the ultimate drag queen.[‡]

Slinking, strutting, prowling, stalking: cat movement has set the standard for femininity in fashion and on the street. Paws pad

---

[‡] See the popular Instagram account @rupaws_drag_race for the receipts.

silently, legs so synchronized they levitate mesmerically. Feline agility—it's otherworldly. Every step so styled it seems they just might be showing off for an audience of human spectators. They don't call it a catwalk for nothing.

Recently, cat women, like witchy women, have become a trendy archetype with a whole new wardrobe for sale. In 2018, the *Wall Street Journal* announced that cat fashion has finally released cat-loving women from the shackles of stigma. "The cat lady cliché is over thanks to new feline fashion," reads the headline of a piece written by Lauren Mechling. "This new breed of unapologetic cat lady that the fashion world is championing intersects, coincidentally or not, with the resurgence of feminism associated with the #metoo movement," she asserts. Now, a wealth of cat-inspired pieces by brands like Balenciaga, Marni, and Louis Vuitton are "recasting cat-printed merchandise as stylish rather than pathetic." Ouch.

Cat ladies have historically been cast as too old or too weird to be stylish, so there is truth to the fact that the resurgence of feminist ideals as part of a new movement for gender equality has made many rethink such sexist assumptions. However, as important as it is to demolish arcane notions about women and cats, buying your way out of it with $1,870 silk cat pajamas (actually a thing, by Louis Vuitton and Grace Coddington, by the way) isn't an accessible or sustainable model for cultural change.

On the other hand, there are a few upsides to such trends. The presence of the witch in popular culture, for example, has arguably inspired neophytes interested in the occult to dig past surface aesthetics, and it may have also removed some of the stigma from practitioners, too. The same can be said for cat ladies. Given the popularity of witches and feminism and the new breed of self-identified cat ladies who are shamelessly open about their affections, it's only natural that these ideas would find their own fashionable expression.

Cat Coven, a line of clothing and accessories designed and produced by witch Kjersti Faret, offers occult-centric feline wear in this vein. Inspired by an interest in the occult, art history, feminism, and cats, Cat Coven offers "accessories and apparel for witches, feminists, and weirdos." When asked why cats pair perfectly with this trifecta, Faret points to a wildness, an inability to be tamed, that they all share.

"Cats are pretty independent and commonly keep to themselves, which adds to their mysteriousness," Faret explains. "I think it also causes a lot of people to feel they don't understand them or can't approach them. . . . Like a witch or a feminist or any outsider from the mainstream, cats are following their own path. They don't conform to your demands. They have their own agenda."

One of Faret's most iconic (and most plagiarized) designs, "Magickal Protection," includes a black cat's brooding countenance inside a braided circle with a pentagram on its forehead. Moon phases float on top, and three crystals sparkle below. Other popular designs center on a warrior cat inspired by Joan of Arc, a priestess of Freya featuring a shaggy cat-headed figure with breasts bared atop a crescent moon, and a Samhain favorite depicting three cats gathered around a bubbling cauldron under a starry night sky. One wears a pointed witch hat; the other two have crescent moons above their eyes and carry esoteric items around their torsos: animal bones, potions. Faret has designed items just for cats, too, like catnip-filled pillows or cat capes that double as human bandannas.

Many of Cat Coven's offerings tend toward the strictly mystical, but Faret doesn't shy away from political messaging that appeals to social justice–minded witches. The shop boasts a "Neo-Nazis Not Welcome" patch that has a fanged cat chomping into the body of a serpent, and another that simply says "Feminism Means Equality. That's It."

Substance is as important as style—particularly when it comes to Cat Coven's means of production. There are all kinds of nuanced discussions to be had about the attendant ethics of production, consumption, labor, and the capitalist system when you're dealing with clothing often made by the hands of women working in sweatshops around the world. Unlike so much of the cat-themed clothing that is produced in sweatshops or designed to be disposable, however, Faret endeavors to use materials that are sustainable and ethical and is transparent on her website about where her materials originate.

"I think about this a lot as a shop owner and human who is creating more physical things to take up space and resources in our world," Faret admits. "I am in a constant struggle between my love of making products and my guilt of not being able to make all my work eco-friendly. I try my best in the broken system we have, but I can always be doing better, which is a big goal for me this year."

Despite the bad rap fashion designers and clothing companies get for exploiting not only natural resources but consumers themselves, Cat Coven exemplifies the kind of business that is as much about serving the community as it is trying to better it. Perhaps being in tune with the animal world in addition to the spiritual world heightens awareness of the interconnectedness between us all. "There's just something so special about having a friendship with an animal from a different species," Faret muses. "To be able to experience a bond with another creature is magic itself."

> **The electric furs of the lynx, panther and even domestic cat were stitched to garments, in imitation of the ancient bacchanalia.**
>
> –Eliphas Levi

The cat is an exercise in aesthetics. Hair teased up erotic or enraged, fur smoothed down clean and calm and cool: there is liberation in tapping into feline glamour magic. Pouring yourself into the provocative patterns of wildcats is an act so ubiquitous nowadays it almost goes unnoticed. And yet, dressing in ways that imitate feline coats or eyes or shapes are everyday rituals of transformation that initiate the wearer into primal, nonverbal embodiment. It has become a power move particularly for women who seek to shift shape into these beasts—or at least temporarily take on a feral attribute or two in the process. These rituals parallel the kind of shamanic practices found around the world where a witch or magician wears the flayed skin of the animal they wish to channel. The fashion industry may offer a stunning variety of ways to embody the feline form, but there's more than one way to skin a cat—or to wear catskin.

When we talk about transformation, the process of becoming catlike has often involved putting on the hides stripped from the backs of living cats. Artemis, Greek goddess of hunting and fertility, was at times depicted wearing a lion's head and skin. Kali, Hindu goddess of creation and destruction, was sometimes said to wear a tiger skin—along with her signature garland of human skulls. The Norse, Saami, and indigenous peoples in North America and Australia all incorporate some form of animal skin into their sacred practices, too.

Frederika Bain explains in *Flaying in the Pre-Modern World* that putting on another being's skin can "facilitate passage to an alternate state of being" and in the process "initiates a mode of border-crossing, becoming a floating threshold between one form of the self and another."

The same kind of sympathetic magic at play in the seemingly mundane act of donning a leopard-print dress is at the heart of these animal-skin rituals. Wearing something that represents or is taken from what you wish to become draws you closer to it.

"Folktales of shape-changing animal/human beings may also stipulate that the change be effected by dressing in the physical skin of the animal into which the human is to turn," Bain elaborates. There is also the belief that wearing a skin taken from an animal isn't necessarily about becoming that animal, she continues, but general border-crossing or shape-shifting between the worlds of (wo)man and beast and different states of consciousness.

Catskin played a part in all kinds of conjuring in pagan Europe.

A group of fourteenth-century French monks and laymen were once caught trying to raise the demon Berich using a circle constructed of catskin. A witch sect in Savoy during the fifteenth century attempted to destroy crops by filling the skin of a cat with vegetable matter. They then spread the concoction's pulverized powder across the land as a sacrifice to the Devil. Sixteenth-century demonologist Bodin wrote in *De la démonomanie des sorciers* that using a pelt of a lion would give one "the power to attract or repel demons." There were also whispers of witches wearing feline cloaks at their sabbaths, too.

At the same time, some Christians were donning catskin, not as a power move, but as a last resort. An English sumptuary law from 1127 stated that abbesses and nuns couldn't wear "garments more precious than those of lambs' wool or of black cat's fur." Another from 1363 forbade yeoman's wives, daughters, and children from wearing fur—unless it was made from lamb, rabbit, fox, or cat.

The devaluing of cat fur and catskin in these instances coincides with an early English version of the Cinderella tale, called "Catskin."

A young woman born to a father who hates her for not being male dons a coat of catskin to run away disguised as a peasant girl. She begins a new life as a scullery maid (and in the nineteenth-century version is repeatedly called a "slut" by the cook she works for in the kitchen). After much hardship, "Catskin," as they call her because of her signature humble cloak, finally finds her prince.

In myth and in magic, feline skin can invoke strength in its wearer and ignite a change of state. When ancient goddesses dressed in the mantle of lions or tigers, worshippers were reminded of their parental and predatory instincts. When nuns or yeomen's wives or proto-Cinderellas wore catskin, their status dropped. When women of today wear feline prints, they can be elevated to sex goddess status—if the price is right—or they can be seen as tacky, low-class, and unfashionable.

Above all, a shift in perception or presence—physical or metaphorical—is guaranteed when you are enveloped in feline fashion.

Sex Kittens and Painted Cats—
Untamed Eroticism

P ainted cats, sex kittens, cathouses—felines and sex workers
have been intimates for hundreds of years. Leaning into sensual pleasure, conjuring alternate modes of survival, and evading
male authority, they have played similar social roles.

As early as the 1700s, artistic depictions of courtesans were
crawling with cats. Felines figure in all kinds of art, but they "are
more common in pictures of witches and in genre scenes featuring
amorous women or prostitutes," writes Laurinda S. Dixon in *Perilous Chastity*.

One prime example is William Hogarth's "A Harlot's Prog-
ress" series of 1731–32, a morality tale that follows the rise and
fall of a girl from the English countryside who moves to London,
becomes a sex worker, and eventually dies of syphilis. The third
engraving takes us into the room of Mary Hackabout after she
finishes with a gentleman caller. She tilts her head toward us with

a coquettish smile, her bodice unlaced just enough so that one of her breasts might heave out at any moment. Behind her, a pointed witch hat and broomstick hang on the wall. Next to her, a maid pours a spot of tea. Beneath her, a cat playfully peeks under the hem of her dress.

In this scene, "the cat serves as part of an image sequence: cat, harlot, witch's hat, and broomstick, signifying *witchcraft* as well as *masquerades* (where whores met clients)," writes Ronald Paulson in *Hogarth's Harlot: Sacred Parody in Enlightenment England*. Cats were not normally kept as pets in 1730s London, so they "must have still carried some of the sense of danger (or bad luck) they had in the times of witchcraft scares," Paulson notes. There has been much illicit magic made in Hackabout's quarters no doubt, despite the encroaching magistrates at the door, on their way to arrest her for merely trying to survive under mercantilism.

Felines signal far more than witchcraft in depictions of sex workers, however. "The cat is the animal aspect of her," Paulson affirms. Often, sex workers would be shown accompanied by dogs, which were stand-ins for their male clients. In this case, the cat is clearly her owner's double, "presumably because a cat in heat will mate with more than one male and attracts males from far and near," he writes. "The harlot's cat has a collar around her neck (she is 'kept'), is sniffing under the harlot's skirt, and has her tail raised in the air, her vulva prominently displayed." Paulson asks: "Is her provocative pose intended to represent the in-heat position? Is it an invitation to be mounted?" Only if the price is right.

In another scene plucked from art history of the eighteenth century, James Gillray's etching from 1779, *The Whore's Last Shift*, depicts a sex worker and her cat. She is standing nude, save for stockings, heels, and an ornate headpiece—the literal height of glamour. As she washes her undergarments by hand in a bowl, an orange striped cat watches her from the window, paw outstretched, perhaps beckoning in solidarity. They've had a long night.

Then there's Édouard Manet's *Olympia*, which scandalized Paris in 1863. *Olympia* is a study in the gaze, with a naked white woman and cat serving similar stares. The two face forward, hard and unbothered, challenging the viewer to accept their wantonness as a black servant is sidelined in the scene. The cat in both these paintings serves as double, but also as an indicator of sexual abandon. The cat's presence represents a woman's wild nature, her willingness to tease and play. The woman's presence draws attention to the cat's wild nature, its instincts to tease and play.

Olympia includes multiple visual cues that connote sex work— the confrontational gaze, the cat, the name Olympia, which was associated with sex workers in 1860s Paris—although the woman who posed for the painting, artist Victorine Meurent, was not a known sex worker. It is the presence of a feline in *Olympia*, and in all the above works, that is the most significant sign about the kind of women these male artists were depicting.

On the other side of the world, sex workers appeared with their feline allies in Japanese ukiyo-e ("pictures of the floating world"). Kaigetsudo Dohan's *Courtesan Playing with a Cat* woodcut print from c. 1715 gives us a window into the relationship between a sex worker and her pet during a moment of lighthearted fun. She dangles a printed handkerchief in front of a black-and-white cat, poised to paw. Nearly a century later, an image by Utagawa Kunisada II from c. 1820–24 shows a courtesan with a toothpick in her mouth similarly playing with her spotted cat.

By the 1840s, the Tokugawa shogunate had banned artists from featuring ne'er-do-wells like kabuki actors, geisha, and courtesans in their work, but Utamaro Kuniyoshi skirted the rule by drawing cats instead. His print *Pale Moon, Cats in Season* from 1846 offers a scene full of cat customers admiring glamorous cat courtesans in elegant kimonos, their whiskers offsetting their come-hither smiles.

The cats/sex worker combo persisted into the twentieth century. In the 1971 film *Klute*, Jane Fonda plays an escort and cuddles her calico in a few salient scenes. In Queen's 1974 hit "Killer Queen," Freddie Mercury sings about an elite call girl he compares to a pussycat. Tina Turner's 1984 song "Private Dancer" about a sex worker features a black cat slinking around her ankles on the album cover.

It's tempting to think that the association between cats and female hustlers has been driven only by a pejorative, patriarchal perspective, but the connection has also been embraced by sex workers for quite some time. In Edo Japan, stories of the shape-shifting cat courtesans known as *bakeneko yujo* who might take a man as a snack permeated local lore. But instead of running from such associations, many courtesans kept cats as pets or chose feline-esque names to cloak themselves in catlike mystery and heighten their dangerously seductive appeal.

Sex workers of today are just as likely to invoke this age-old association in their work and aesthetic. When I put out a call to interview sex workers who used cat imagery or role-play in their sessions, the response was overwhelming. Some women starred in porn scenes pretending to be naughty, horny kitties, some did BDSM role-play where they became slinky feline tops, some said wearing wildcat prints was the key to *slut*cess, and everyone had theories about why cats and sex workers make such bosom buddies.

"They're sexy animals," porn performer Arabelle Raphael tells me in a phone conversation. (She describes herself as a cat lady whose "high femme clothes are covered in cat hair.") When asked what she thinks the connection between cats and sex workers is, she reveals that she's intuited the connection since her teens. "They are the aspirational sex worker," she explains. "They make you work to get it."

On her OnlyFans clips site, Raphael offers multiple scenes for purchase where she plays a cat. In one subtly sensual scene, she is a mom who suddenly transforms into a kitty for her daughter to play with. In another more explicit clip, she purrs and chirps and rolls around on all fours, turning into a cat who finds pleasure with a pink vibrator. With whiskers and a heart-shaped black nose painted on her face, she wears a bell on a collar, cat ears tied with ribbons, and a butt plug with a furry tail on the other end.

Comedian and stripper Jacqueline Frances, aka Jacq the Stripper, finds the links between cats and sex work obvious, likening strip clubs to cat cafés. "You have to sit there and you have to let the cats come to you," she says over brunch one day. "You can try to go after the cats, but you might get scratched."

Jacq has even worked this dynamic into her merchandise. One popular pin she sells is a pink cat slyly displaying its asshole—depicted as a dollar sign—as it smirks at an imaginary audience. "I always thought a cat's display of their asshole is so pronounced, and when I learned how important asshole confidence was in sex work, I just drew that picture one day," she says matter-of-factly.

Jo Weldon, sex worker, activist, burlesque dancer, and author of *Fierce: The History of Leopard Print*, has been serving up wildcat energy for decades. A Leo born in the Year of the Tiger, she wore her scarlet hair in an expansive, teased lion's mane in the 1980s when she began dancing at strip clubs with names like The Classic Cat and The Cheetah. Since early childhood, Weldon has identified with cats—and witches, too. "It felt really natural; I felt like it was for me," she says. "I like the idea of being nocturnal.

Cats are fun-loving and they're mysterious at the same time. They're unknowable, lovable jerks. I'm always interested in anything that has an obvious dichotomous meaning."

A beacon for bestial burlesque, Weldon's performances and productions have, over the years, involved a variety of cat numbers. She's been a black cat fighting off a foe, a lion overflowing with hunt energy, and a sadistic tiger (that show ended with her pulling out the sequined guts of another performer). For Weldon's fifty-sixth birthday she even staged a "cathouse" burlesque show and invited fellow performers to interpret that as they wished.

It was a popular theme, to say the least.

The aesthetics and attitudes we associate with cats today have been infused into sex work for centuries. But if art, history, and the words of contemporary sex workers still don't have you convinced of these hallowed links, I offer up twelve strip clubs named with wildcats and kittens in mind. If you happen to visit any of them, just a word to the wise: as Jacq the Stripper so graciously reminds us, consent is queen, and the way you'd approach a cat (or let them approach you!) isn't so different from engaging with a stripper you wish to patronize.

1. Cheetahs (Los Angeles, CA)

2. Kittens Cabaret (Seattle, WA)

3. Kittens Gentlemen's Club (Salisbury, MA)

4. Candy Cat Too (Winnetka; CA)

5. Polekatz (Bridgeview, IL)

6. Sassy Kats Showclub (Indianapolis, IN)

7. Catwalk of Memphis (Memphis, TN)

8. Miss Kitty (Washington Park, IL)

9. Exotic Kitty Gentlemen's Club (Salt Lake City, UT)

10. The Red Leopard (Satellite Beach, FL)

11. Tiger Cabaret (Dallas, TX)

12. Tiger Tail Lounge (Rockford, IL)

The Black Cat

I do identify very much with the black cat," dominatrix Dia Dynasty tells me inside a yurt covered in white fur throws. There is an altar space adorned with crystals, candles, and divination tools on one side of the enclosure, and her black cat slinks in as we speak. "They are seen as maybe unlucky or less desirable to people who are superstitious about 'the weird one,'" she continues, gesturing to her familiar. "I have a lot of tattoos. I do talk about magic and witchcraft in a very open way."

A witch in her personal and professional life, Dynasty is cofounder of New York City dungeon La Maison du Rouge and practices "transformational domination," which she defines as bringing in "elements of healing and energetics—stuff that's a little more metaphysical than just sex." At times, she has incorporated cat play into her sessions, but for the most part, Dynasty simply embodies the feral feminine, as opposed to consciously behaving or dressing like a cat. "There is a mystery to me," she smiles, her pin-straight bangs falling in an eldritch curtain across her forehead. "I could easily turn, claws out."

In legend and folklore, black cats are larger than life, and they're often attributed a kind of spellbinding eroticism with a hint of ferocity that those like Dia have in spades. Out at night, or hiding in plain sight, bringing bad luck or blessings, as path crossers or misfortune blockers: the black cat is a potent symbol of the outcast and outlier. They've been slinky vagabonds, ruthless vigilantes, astral projections of evil, and sibyls of self-reliance.

The kind of femininity that pervades black cat lore is brought to life in Kaneto Shindo's *Kuroneko* (which translates to "black cat"). In this 1968 rape-revenge film, it is a black cat that helps women transcend their trauma. Set in Heian-era Japan, the opening credits roll with a thick mist snaking through a bamboo forest as drums pound and a cackle reverberates through the trees. Soon, a roving band of samurai appears and approaches the humble home of a mother and her daughter. They begin to ransack the place, terrorizing them in the process. By the time the men leave, the house is ablaze, and the women have been brutally raped and murdered.

As their bodies lie amid the smoking ruins, a black cat creeps toward their remains. It yowls ominously and begins to crawl across the two, licking their lips and wounds. Flash-forward to the future, and the mother and daughter are alive again, exacting their revenge by charming passing samurai into their homes and to their deaths.

Since their encounter with the black cat, both women have become visions of ghostly appeal, the daughter in particular. The men don't know what to make of her elegant hands that suddenly seem to feature black fur or her eyes that transform into a yellow cat's stare. With feline ferocity—and the help of her mother—the daughter systematically seduces the samurai before sinking her teeth into their throats, sucking them dry.

Although this duo is certainly a man's worst nightmare, they aren't merely the reflections of patriarchal fears. In "Ghosts of Desire," Colette Balmain argues that the two "might well be symbols of male desire and projections of male anxiety, but at the same time they offer a mode of empowerment outside traditional binaries," she writes. Unlike other similar horror films in the *bakeneko mono* (monster-cat tales) subgenre, the women "call into question the discourses around femininity, respectability, and passivity." They have found their own ways to thrive within appalling circumstances.

Sex and violence are often part of the black cat's oeuvre: the vampiress Carmilla appears as a black cat to suck the life out of her beloved in bed. Lilith, the MVP of demons, becomes a big, blood-sucking black cat in Spanish Jewish folklore known as El Broosha. Chordeva, a witch who takes the form of a black cat in Bengalese belief, wields death in the tip of her sandpaper tongue. Then there's Catwoman, of course—most often shown with black cats, not tabbies or calicoes.

But the black cat isn't limited to the realm of the erotic.

In a piece for the anthology *Becoming Dangerous: Witchy Femmes, Queer Conjurers, and Magical Rebels,* writer Maranda Elizabeth describes the process of becoming a black cat for self-protection. "One of my visualizations for getting around the city is to imagine myself, my crooked body and odd appearance, as a black cat crossing somebody's path: good luck to some, bad luck to others," they write in "Trash-Magic: Signs & Rituals for the Unwanted."

The self-described "amethyst-femme" recounts their habit of traipsing across the city, cane in hand, encountering cats in moments of kinship as they collect refuse for sustenance and for ritual.

"As I prowl through the streets searching for food and treasure," Elizabeth writes, "those black cats, who appear as symbols of my own strength, luck, and survival, don't just cross my path, don't just share a furtive glance and saunter away." Instead, the cats see their reflection in human form, too, and are eager to greet their sibling. "Their tails spiral and swirl around my body and then around my cane, and I realise my cane is my own tail, too: the magical fifth limb giving me stability and presence, giving me access," Elizabeth muses.

Black cats are Elizabeth's brethren, living outside normative social structures and strictures. Both are "underappreciated misfit creatures who cultivate a sense of belonging wherever they go."

The black cat is nothing if not a misfit.

Black cats have been set apart from other felines as far back as ancient Egypt. The color black and black cats themselves were associated with Isis, the great mother goddess, as well as Bastet, who also wielded maternal powers. To Egyptians, black symbolized death and the afterlife, as well as regeneration, rejuvenation, and fertility. Some believed that they would gain favor with Bastet if they hosted a black cat in their homes. This association shifted for the ancient Greeks— even though they would adopt Egyptian goddesses like Isis into their pantheon—and black became synonymous with evil and the underworld, which was demarcated from the land of the living by the river Acheron, whose waters ran dark as night. By the fifth century BC, black cats were understood to be harbingers of misfortune, at least according to the play *The Ecclesiazusae* by Aristophanes, which has the line: "That an earthquake may come or an ill-omened flash of lightning, that a black cat may run across the street . . ."

The Romans carried on the Greek association of black cats with death and the underworld, as Bastet/Isis informed their vision of Hecate, goddess of the underworld, who was, of course, a shape-shifter and necromancer. Hecate was linked with Artemis, the virgin goddess of motherhood and fertility and the ruler of beasts, who at one point herself turned into a cat, according to Antoninus Liberalis's *Metamorphoses*. This winding mythological road would continue into Europe centuries later, when *Vox in Rama* and similar ecclesiastical writings further damned black cats as satanic and the witch's accomplice.

Given their storied connection to the underworld, black cats were alas commonly used as ingredients in devious magical workings. Saint Cyprian's spell from the third century to "execute extreme vengeance" involved tying up a pure-black cat with no trace of white fur at a crossroads and ordering the Devil to enter the body of an enemy, thereby binding the Dark Lord to the body of that enemy as the cat has been bound. Black cats were also part of more mundane spells, like Cornelius Agrippa's spell for divorce, which involved a seal of red copper perfumed with the hair of a black dog and the hair of a black cat. As mentioned in chapter 7, hoodoo rituals of all kinds involved black cat body parts, too.

Black cats were also known to appear as apparitions of vengeance. In fact, occultist Dion Fortune was once attacked by the astral projections of black cats for publishing accounts on the abuses inherent in occult fraternities.

"We became most desperately afflicted with black cats," she explains in *Psychic Self-Defense*. "They were not hallucinatory cats, for our neighbors shared in the affliction, and we exchanged commiserations with the caretaker next door who was engaged in pushing bunches of black cats off doorstep and window-sill with a broom, and declared he had never in his life seen so many, or such dreadful specimens. . . . We looked out of the window, and the street as far as we could see was dotted with black cats and they were wailing and howling in broad daylight as they do on the roofs at night."

After this harrowing experience, Fortune performed an exorcism, and the cats were gone as mystically as they had arrived. She hardly forgot them, however, as they would become the inspiration for her classic book about protecting oneself from psychic invasion.

Evil or good, masculine or feminine, feted or feared, black cats have appeared on every side of the story, but outdated associations die hard. Superstition still impacts these black beauties, which has inspired animal shelters to signal boost Black Cat Appreciation Day on August 17 and National Black Cat Day on October 27, as raven-hued cats tend to be adopted with less frequency. Even as I wrote this book, I encountered a neighbor in my building who was apprehensive when she heard I was getting a new kitten. Her eyes narrowed as she said she hoped it wasn't black. I smiled and assured her there were much more frightening things than a little black housecat.

Bloody Kisses—
Vampires, Werecats, and Cat People

Black lips peel to reveal two white fangs. Hissing, kissing, they sink into fresh flesh. A bloody tide is lapped. Gushing turns to a leak, then dries into a crimson crust along the corners of a grinning mouth. Not a witch but a bloodsucker, cats are vampires, too.

As far as Hollywood is concerned, witches and vampires are distinct. Witches, we're told, are of the earth. They work earthly magic and cast otherworldly spells. They are old women; they are young women (rarely men). They are broom-riding wood dwellers or upscale city slickers, vagabonds acting out of malice and/or sexual abandon.

Vampires are not entirely of the earth in the sense that earthly remedies are their kryptonite: garlic, sunlight. Their spellcasting comes in the form of coaxing a victim into bloodletting or, rather, inviting them in to feast on their fluids. Vampires may be more stereotypically male, but female vampires range from children to youthful babes to powerful, experienced women with allure in spite of (or because) they are just past their prime. They are rarely the crones we associate with the prototypical witch.

Despite their differences, in the Venn diagram of witches and vampires there is quite an overlap.§ Both witches and vampires are wont to seduce their victims through some sort of erotic hypnotic. Their methods differ, but they are united in a rich history that's punctuated by tales of their ghastly appetites—and taking feline form.

Female witches and vampires, according to film theorist Barbara Creed, belong in the "monstrous-feminine" category. Libidinous tales of murderous witches were commonplace in early modern Europe, but vampires have quite the libido too, says Creed. "The female vampire is abject because she disrupts identity and order; driven by her lust for blood, she does not respect the dictates of the law which set down the rules of proper sexual conduct." The same can be said of the witch. But although the witch's drive is often a metaphorical lust for blood, that is not always the case, especially when she takes on feline form.

In the early fifteenth century, two women were executed in the Pyrenees for supposedly breaking into homes in the form of cats and drinking the blood of all the children they could find inside.

Italy and the Slavic countries were also fixated upon vampiric witches. In Croatia, witches were thought to tear at the flesh of babies, but in the form of cats, they would drink the blood of adults.

According to Ronald Hutton in *The Witch*, our Enlightenment ideas about vampires might have actually developed out of witch folklore of the early modern era. "The special characteristic of the

---

§ Archetypally speaking, of course, because witches are indeed real, but vampires? I'm not so sure (although a lot of goth clubs I've frequented would beg to differ).

modern vampire, as a bloodsucker, may indeed have developed from this concept of the witch, as it came to be applied to the restless dead in the eighteenth century," he writes.

From a behavioral perspective, though, vampires are far more catlike than witches. Vampires are stealthy and nocturnal. Vampires can live numerous "lives." Vampires are carnivorous and lust for the hunt; they do their deeds in close quarters, intimately. There is no escaping the pressing of the flesh, no hexing from afar, no application of sympathetic magic to avoid the touch and taste and smell of their victims.

Although the classic vampire figure has been a pallid man with a brusque, Eastern European accent and billowing cape who can turn into a bat, one foundational vampire novel was actually about a lesbian who took the shape of a frightful black cat to terrorize her victims.

Carmilla, by Joseph Sheridan Le Fanu, was first published in 1871, predating Bram Stoker's *Dracula* by over twenty years. The novella is set in a fictional manor in the countryside and follows the passionate, emotional affair between a young vampiress and another girl, Laura, on whom she has set her sights. Laura, in the bloom of pubescent youth, is drawn to this magnetic, withholding figure whose beauty knows no bounds.

At first, Carmilla appears to be a young woman who has suffered a bout of illness and is merely in need of a place to rest and recuperate. Laura, an only child whose mother died some years before, becomes enthralled with the way Carmilla moves, the way she dresses, the way she treats her.

"It was like the ardor of a love," Laura recalls, "with gloating eyes she drew me to her, and her hot lips traveled along my cheek in kisses; and she would whisper, almost in sobs, 'You are mine, you *shall* be mine, you and I are one forever.'"

Carmilla follows these moments of erotic bombast with bratty silent spells and cavalier bon mots about death. Laura is confused by Carmilla's erratic moods, unsure why this mysterious stranger lavishes so much attention upon her and then refuses to open up emotionally. She is at once repelled and attracted by the stirrings of romance that begin to bubble up.

Once Carmilla ingratiates herself into Laura and her father's lives, she slowly begins to bleed the life out of her new bestie. Laura becomes increasingly despondent. She is lovesick and lost, addicted to Carmilla's affections with a singular focus. One night she awakes to see a horrifying feline entity approaching. It was "a sooty-black animal that resembled a monstrous cat," Laura explains. "I felt it spring lightly on the bed. The two broad eyes approached my face, and suddenly I felt a stinging pain as if two large needles darted, an inch or two apart, deep into my breast. I waked with a scream." She then sees the figure of a woman dissolve before she is alone again and can catch her breath.

After this bloody consummation, Laura and her father eventually find out from a family friend that another young girl has also been seduced—and killed—by an outrageous flirt named Millarca. Millarca, we come to see, is Carmilla. A mere shuffling of letters has allowed her to take on a new identity, and she undergoes yet another, final, state change when she meets her bloody end at the hands of Laura's father.

The horror of female sexuality and the female body spreads like a contagion throughout Le Fanu's tale, as the author invokes the parallel evils of hysteria, homosexuality, and vampirism. Although the word *hysteric* is never used in *Carmilla*, there is a fair amount of time devoted to Carmilla's mystery illness, which includes irregular sleeping habits, lack of appetite, and great anxiety—which Laura slowly picks up. The two bond over their ailments in a way—one could even imagine a radical rewriting of the tale featuring the queer lovers reading Johanna Hedva's "Sick Woman Theory" to each other in bed.

The hysteric, who was long believed to suffer mental anguish because of an unruly uterus, is like the vampire, whose lust is also perverted and expressed in unfathomable ways. In *The New Nineteenth Century: Feminist Readings of Underread Victorian Fiction*, Tamar Heller cites an 1877 writing on the treatment of hysteria that suggests hysterics create other hysterics. "A hysterical girl is . . . a vampire who sucks the blood of the healthy people about her," physician Weir Mitchell explains. "Pretty surely where there is one hysterical girl there will soon or late be two sick women." Using *Carmilla* as an apt example, Heller explains how "both the female hysteric and the female vampire embody a relation to desire that the nineteenth-century culture finds highly problematic."

In addition to hysteria and homosexuality, Carmilla is also abject because of her animality. Patriarchal myths have consistently ascribed women with primal animal characteristics and men with the foresight and ability to vanquish them. Bram Dijkstra's analysis of *Carmilla* in *Idols of Perversity: Fantasies of Feminine Evil in Fin-de-Siècle Culture* posits that "evil in this narrative is the never-ending evil of all women—their blood link with the animal past."

But although Carmilla may literally embody the feline fatale, her capricious character also reflects another recurring aspect of the feral feminine. According to Linda Ruth Williams in *Critical Desire: Psychoanalysis and the Literary Subject*, the vampire rejects the "binary, waking world" that orders the lives of the living. "Like all good vampires, [Carmilla] is anything but stable, shape-shifting with an uncanny changeability, from solid into vapour, from languid passivity to feline predation."

She defies fixity at all points.

○ ◆ ○

Just as bloodthirsty witches were thought to take cat form during the witch trials, the first female vampire elected feline flesh to find her way into bedrooms at night. As we'll discover, sex-starved feline shape-shifters are a distinct group unto themselves, which begs the question: what other beings might belong to this bestial category? After witches and vampires, there is but one major character left: the werewolf—or, werecat.

Equaling, if not surpassing, the lusty cravings of vampires and witches, werecats are tied to profound levels of sexual deviance. They are perversion incarnate in the films *Sleepwalkers* and *Cat People*, as well as in Margaret Atwood's short story "Lusus Naturae." These human-wildcat hybrids go to great lengths to satiate their libidinal hunger and to slake their thirst.

Atwood's short story, published in the *Stone Mattress: Nine Wicked Tales* collection, is about a young girl afflicted with a mystery disease. Her eyes become yellow and her teeth pink, and whiskers sprout from her face and swathes of black hair cover her chest and arms. Fearful for her safety, her parents let her live locked in her room sustained only by the love of the family cat—and a daily bowl of blood her mother brings her.

"He was the only living creature who wanted to be close to me," she says of the cat. "I smelled of blood, old dried up blood: perhaps that was why he shadowed me, why he would climb up onto me and start licking." She describes her nocturnal habits, when she would leave her room and prowl around outside, mewing and growling at strangers in the dark to spook them, hunting and eating chickens.

While out of the house, she comes upon a young man and woman having sex in the woods, gnashing their teeth, biting one another, and making the same growls as she does. Although they look nothing like her, she is confused albeit taken with their lovemaking, and believes they might be in the midst of changing into what she is. After they finish, she comes upon the man, sleeping in the grass, "as if laid out on a platter."

She digs in and lays what she means to be a kiss upon his neck.

When word gets out about her love attack, a swarm of people head toward her house with stakes and torches. "I'm afraid it's bad news for the cat," she warns. "Whatever they do to me, they'll do to him as well."

The protagonist's yearning to experience those first sparks of pleasure that so many pubescent girls desire is, in the end, what does her in. The more she is kept from human intimacy, the more she craves it. Her urges are ultimately violent, although in her innocence she doesn't mean them to be.

This gendered symbolism—an adolescent girl devouring an adolescent boy—taps into well-worn narratives about monstrous femininity. It's that sexual evil that supposedly awakens from a demonic slumber during puberty: when young girls start getting cast as sexual sorceresses, luring in older men, hypnotizing male peers, asking for *it*, and being blamed for a host of sexist desires and assumptions they never had a hand in creating. Ironically, it is the desires of teenage males that are more likely to court violent endings, but the fear of budding female sexuality has consistently been a societal scapegoat.

One proposed "solution" to this so-called "problem" of female sexuality is to close your eyes and hope nothing bad will happen. Just like abstinence-only sex education, however, we know that never really works. As the film *Cat People* shows, ignoring it only makes things worse.

First released in 1942 (and remade in 1982), *Cat People* explores the horror of female desire. In the first film, a young, soft-spoken Serbian woman, Irena, hails from a race of witches who shape-shift into werecats because of a satanic curse. When they are aroused or angered, nothing can stop them from devouring their lovers alive.

The intensity of the film lies in its tension. Irena suppresses her physical need for her new husband Oliver while she shudders with longing, barely able to restrain herself. He's equally concerned with their relationship's lack of consummation, but chalks it up to shyness or trauma or "woman-stuff" (typical 1940s fare).

One scene puts the newly betrothed on either side of a door, seething through the barrier that keeps them from indulging in forbidden flesh. It is both a metaphorical and literal animal within her champing at the bit to be given free rein (which harkens back to those retrograde ideas about hysterics and the wildcats within their wombs). Irena runs her hands like claws down the door as a panther, locked away in the zoo nearby, yowls into the night air.

The first *Cat People* film became a curious hit in part because "the central motif is fear of sex, and specifically a woman's fear of the ravenous sexuality she's been conditioned to suppress," writes Michael Barrett in *PopMatters*. Forty years later, the second film takes this theme to even darker extremes.

This time, virginal Irena has a brother who is also a werecat. Every time he has sex, he transforms into a panther and must kill someone to return to human form. To remedy this required carnage, he tells Irena that she should dump her boyfriend and they should submit to an incestuous relationship, which won't kill anyone. This, unsurprisingly, horrifies her, despite finding out that her parents, now dead, were also brother and sister.

Irena does succumb to lust at the end of this twisted tale, but is able to suppress her animal instincts so her beloved (a zookeeper) doesn't have to die. Instead of killing to regain her humanity post-sex, she chooses to live on in panther form behind bars as a kept woman—his pet—stroked and fed by his hand. It's a fitting punishment for the girl who gives in.

Incest remains a theme in the 1992 werecat classic, Stephen King's *Sleepwalkers*. The camp favorite opens silently with a definition of one type of werecat, sourced from the (fictional) *Chillicoathe Encyclopaedia of Arcane Knowledge* from 1884. "Sleepwalker," it reads, "nomadic, shape-shifting creatures with human and feline origins. Vulnerable to the deadly scratch of the cat, the sleepwalker feeds upon the life-force of virginal human females. Probable source of the vampire legend."

Although in reality witch folklore is the source of vampire legend, these words set the stage for a scintillating tale of werecats gone wild. Within the first five minutes of the film, we're privy to a mother and her teenage son slow dancing, flirting, slow grinding, and then dashing off, breathless, to the bedroom.

Unlike the cat in Margaret Atwood's story, cats in *Sleepwalkers* are enemies, not allies. The werecat may be a fun-house version of a cat, but the domesticated felines go for the jugular when fighting back against these creatures. Cats are the true heroes of the film—and the comic relief. Dozens of adorable felines meow patiently while lolling on the lawn outside the Sleepwalker household, calmly waiting for one to walk outside so they can sink their claws in.

The forbidden sexuality in Stephen King's film, as in *Cat People*, is the familial boundary violation of incest. Young female sexuality is also given weight in the story, too. So much power is accorded to women unsullied by sex, in fact, that virginity is the only thing these abominable cats can live on.

Witches, vampires, and werecats are shape-shifters that can transcend their physical forms, but they are also the embodiment of an immutable fear of sex for the sake of pure pleasure, sex that challenges reproductive roles and family ties.

"Shape-shifters act upon their socially transgressive impulses, thereby providing a vicarious psychological release," explains Brent A. Stypczynski in *The Modern Literary Werewolf*. "Said impulses include wildness, violence, nudity taboos, bestiality . . . , adultery, and rape," he writes. "By blaming the transgressive violence and sex on the beast, the human part of the individual is absolved even as it is punished."

We run to and recoil from these unsettling feline tales to take solace in what we're not—and sometimes to find comfort in what we are.

Tricksters, Shifters, and Femmes Fatales

Feminine shape-shifters wander between worlds—human and animal, natural and supernatural—never fully alighting on one for too long. Catwoman, Carmilla, the *gnaghe*, and all the cat shape-shifters we've met thus far are defined by these itinerant paths. The shape-shifter archetype has proven to be well-suited for those trying to transcend trauma and the circumstances they were born into, but can archetypes become limiting, and when do they devolve into stereotypes?

Resplendent or repellent, beautiful or brainy, virgin or whore: archetypes and stereotypes can trap women into confining dualities. Consider the witch: an empowering archetype to magical practitioners and political revolutionaries alike, or a green-faced, claw-handed warty woman who cackles and casts malicious spells? She most certainly falls into stereotype territory. The cat-woman, too, shares both stereotypical and archetypal attributes, whether you imagine her morphing from wicked witch into devious feline, vampire into blood-sucking cat, or mild-mannered Selina Kyle into Catwoman.

Although archetypes are usually exemplary figures and stereotypes oversimplified ones, there is nevertheless an uncomfortable overlap between the two. Exploring broad-brush icons of femininity can be useful to understand how women and femininity have historically been conceived by men, by each other, and by themselves—but there can be unfortunate side effects.

As Rebecca Copeland suggests in "Mythical Bad Girls," archetypes "tend to elide the distinction between woman as reality and woman as concept." This process flattens, distorts, and can even erase women's humanity because archetypes "are premised—not on actual nature but on nature perceived."

Granted, lived experiences aren't part of the construction of any archetype for any gender, but in a male-dominated society where women are still fighting to achieve bodily autonomy and equal rights, this lack of dimension is far more detrimental to women, folks on the feminine spectrum, and femininity overall.

"Containing women within archetypes of evil was one measure by which female power was controlled," Copeland cautions. The witch, the whore, the femme fatale: these are the archetypal women we have been taught to fear or fight, whether their danger lurks outside or within ourselves.

But one archetype associated with the feminine and the feline may well shatter the constraints of archetypes and stereotypes altogether: the shape-shifter. The shape-shifter archetype not only allows for but is defined by change. And psychoanalyst Carl Jung and comparative mythologist Joseph Campbell both believed the shape-shifter to be a central part of the human experience.

To Jung, shape-shifting was one attribute of the trickster, a figure prominent in mythologies around the world. Tricksters hold knowledge that others do not and use their wiles to flout convention and outwit those around them. They decenter the status quo and, in the process, often reconfigure systems of power—or at least reveal the mechanisms that drive them.

Norse mythology famously has Loki, who switched genders and species freely; West African lore has Anansi, the trickster god; and some indigenous tribes in what is now western North America have the coyote figure. These well-known tricksters are still defined by their proximity to masculinity, though, which is where the split between tricksters and shape-shifters proves useful when we seek to understand feminine shape-shifters.

In *The Hero with a Thousand Faces*, Joseph Campbell makes room for both the trickster and the shape-shifter as separate archetypes, although they share certain characteristics. The shape-shifter's relationship to the eternal male protagonist Campbell deems "the hero" is different from the trickster's. While the trickster's actions will cause the hero to change his perceptions about the world around him, the shape-shifter's actions will cause "the hero" to change his perceptions about the world in addition to his impressions of the shape-shifter.

Maria Nikolajeva further theorizes about the relationship between tricksters and shape-shifters as it applies to cats in literature. She suggests in "Devils, Demons, Familiars, Friends: Towards a Semiotics of Literary Cats" that "the male trickster cat" differs from the female cat, who is "connected to feminine witchcraft, shape-shifting, mystery, and sexuality." Gender can thus be mapped onto distinctions between the trickster and shape-shifter, which is why the femme fatale is often a shape-shifter. This connection dates back to the *Odyssey* when Odysseus encounters the seductive and nefarious Circe, who serves as a catalyst for growth and inspiration while remaining an untrustworthy ally flitting between friend, lover, and foe. "Circe is the archetype in demonological discussions of transformation," affirms Gareth Roberts in "The Descendents of Circe."

However, shape-shifters don't have to follow these pejorative parameters. That's the beauty of the shape-shifter, really.

Rosalyn Greene explains in *The Magic of Shapeshifting* that there are more than literary and archetypal shape-shifters. There are "animal people" she calls "shifters," who "'shift' into their power animal or totem, astrally, mentally, or in some other way. This ranges from those shifters who practice spirit journeys and those who work with familiars and animal spirit guides," Greene elaborates, "in addition to mental shifters, and even, some say, physical shifters." Those who work specifically with cats—or become them—have distinct qualities too. "Cat shifters are feminine, coy, silent, proud, and full of ancient mysteries and secrets," Greene writes.

The cat itself is born a shape-shifter, literally flexing form at will, but this aspect of *felininity* is intensified when the feline and the feminine meet. Whether the shape-shifter accesses the feline through costume or magic or spiritual practice doesn't matter. Above all, a feline shape-shifter is defined by her transience, her inability to be fully figured out, even by those who seek to codify feminine archetypes in the name of empowerment.

Change is her only constant.

Ailuromancy–Divination with Cats

The *Road to Nowhere Oracle Deck* is fanned out across my hardwood floor. Two white paws creep closer to the pile. With a ginger step, a pink nose sniffs the edge of one, then another. A tongue flicks out. A jaw opens, and a hesitant canine bites the corner. My kitten, Cherie, connects with the card before stepping back to survey the geometric designs before her. I flip over the one she chose: Possession.

I have never, ever, thought to give my cat a tarot reading. Despite experiencing profound personal benefits from ritual and witchcraft, it never once crossed my mind. When I heard that witch, art advisor, and tarot reader Sarah Potter did readings for people and their pets, however, I was emboldened to try.

Sarah is a kinetic burst of color and light. On the night of our appointment, she shows up at my apartment in a hot pink faux fur coat, an evening gown, and slippers, her signature deep turquoise and seafoam mermaid hair framing her animated face.

Intrigued by our colorful visitor, Cherie is cautious but present. She comes out to peek at the cards Sarah has shuffled, and then hides again, eyeing us while ensconced in the bed skirt. As we wait for the cat to get accustomed to the new energy in the room, I ask Sarah when she started reading for animals. She's been doing so casually for years, she tells me, but as the current witch revival sweeps us all up into its current, there have been more and more professional outlets for her skills.

"People are really seeking connection now," she affirms. "People want connections in every sense, with people, with spirituality, with their pets, with their families." And although customers with all kinds of animals have booked her for readings, she believes cats, in particular, have much to teach us—particularly women.

"I feel like cats really let us know their feelings and their needs and their desires, very unapologetically," Sarah says as Cherie pokes her silver-streaked head out from under the bed. (She notes that dogs, on the other hand, are trained to suppress their animal instincts.) "I think it's very easy, especially for women, to think that they can't openly desire something or show a voracious appetite for anything at all, whether it's sex or food or money."

Cats aren't ashamed to ask for treats, Sarah elaborates, or for food or for love, and they let you know what they need, at *every single moment* of every day. "That's an important lesson, to make sure you're taking care of yourself," Sarah explains. "What I really love about a lot of cats is that they don't give a fuck."

She shuffles the oracle cards and lays them down in a pile near Cherie. When she does pet readings, Sarah usually lets the animal paw or peck at a single card and then interprets it. What does she make of the Possession card, I ask? Although one of the last cats she read for also picked the same one, she decided that the straightforward context made sense for him, being a bit of a hellion. But

Cherie? With a plush coat and a total princess vibe, she just likes the finer things in life—you know, *possessions*.

Next, Sarah shuffles her tarot deck for a much longer tarot reading for me and Cherie, who is watching from afar. The first card she draws is the Wheel of Fortune, followed by the Star. "This feels like a true cosmic connection," Sarah smiles, commenting upon the good fortune it was for me to have found Cherie as I was working on this book. (My household's previous cat, Pickles, passed nine months before.) "I think the Star is a card that can mean a lot of different things, but being next to the Wheel of Fortune it just really feels like she's a star to you and you're a star to her, too," she says.

The Queen of Staffs appears next. In many decks—including the Smith-Waite—the card features two lions and a little black cat at the queen's feet. Quite auspicious.

"I really feel like that's her," Sarah says pointing to the regal countenance, "she's so cute and has such a presence. For me, in readings this card feels very much like a queen of inspiration, and I feel like it's quite timely that she comes into your life while you're working on this book."

"I know you know this," Sarah continues, "but I feel like she's providing drive and inspiration, and I can't imagine you finishing this book without her here, without a cat presence. How would you be truly inspired? How were you even doing it without her?"

I couldn't, of course. And so *Cat Call* is dedicated to Cherie Purrie.

Cats have long been perceived as channels for the spirits, as emissaries of the moon's mysteries, as guides to other realms. They have much to teach humans about embodiment and intuition, and so cat divination can be found in a variety of magical traditions. Ailuromancy, also known as felidomancy, is examining a cat's behavior for clues about future events. English lore, for example, produced a variety of weather predictors related to cats that still persist in certain parts of America. If a cat sneezes, they say, it's a sign of rain to come, or if a cat sits with its back to the fire, it's going to snow.

For feline-inclined cartomancers, there are ways cats can become part of their workings, too. Cat oracle decks and tarot decks proliferate, from *Cat Gurus, Spirit Cats, Cat Land,* and *Cat-chy* to the *Considerate Cat,* the *Tarot of Pagan Cats,* the *Tarot of the Cat People,* the *Cat's Eye Tarot,* the *Marseille Cat* deck, *Lady Black* Cat tarot, and the *Cat-rot.* These decks are infused with some elements of feline magic through imagery and design but are no substitute for inviting actual cats to be part of your divination practice.

Sabrina Scott, author of *Witchbody* and a professional tarot reader for over eighteen years, recently designed a cat tarot spread that harnesses cat magic at its most vital. Her "Cat's Choice Spread" appears in the pages of Ignota Books' *Daily Diary 2019* and requires an animal partner to unlock its potential.

Scott designed this three-card spread to be laid out like a feline face, with two cards spaced apart on top to represent the ears, and another centered beneath the two to represent the eyes, nose, and mouth.

"Part of the point of this spread is to really sit with and accept that sometimes we don't know what's best for us," Scott writes in the introduction to the spread. "Cats have so much intelligence and intuition of their own to share with us: mine always seem to know when I'm sad and in need of a little extra care and affection."

To begin, Scott suggests shuffling your deck while keeping in mind the issue or problem you'd like to address through the reading. "Once you feel finished, spread your tarot cards face-down on your bedspread, on the floor, on your altar—wherever you're reading. If your cats are like mine, it won't take them too long to saunter over and start sniffing things out! That may mean stepping all over your cards, licking them, turning them over. Allow your cat(s) to choose the cards for you. You may decide that means whichever cards they step on or touch first, or only if they're able to turn it over themselves, or clearly pull it towards them. Be open to collaborating with your cat on this decision!"

The first card you'll draw with the help of your cat is the Cat's Face Card, and an "overview/summary of the problem." The next card you'll draw is the Left Ear Card, which offers the best intellectual approach to the problem. Finally, the third card you'll draw is the Right Ear Card, which provides the best intuitive approach to the problem.

"Ground yourself and come back to the first card drawn, the cat's face card in all its challenges and provocations," Scott continues, "and sit with the bigger picture. If you've been given a clear choice between two courses of action, perhaps your feline friend will point to (or step on!) the card that shows the best course of action."

Sought out for her no-bullshit, intuitive approach to readings, Scott doesn't mince words when it comes to discussing the principles that guide her witchcraft. Although she did create this cat spread at the behest of Ignota and has an incredibly symbiotic relationship with her cats, she doesn't consider them her familiars as some might assume.

"My cats hang out and help when I'm doing magic sometimes, sometimes they don't," she tells me, "sometimes they just hang and don't help. I personally don't think it's very ethical for me to force them into any form of participating, and therefore I don't consider them to be 'familiars.' I know their understanding of everything is different from mine and that's amazing. If anything, I am *their* familiar, not the other way around. I am in no way 'above' them just because I am human. I don't order them around. They share their presence and energy with me."

Like many of the practitioners I interviewed who have cats in their homes, Scott does reveal that her cats are curious about her workings and do come sniffing around. "I let them participate and hang out as they wish, and they have a healthy respect for magic and for the spirits," she explains.

Above all, Scott believes it's not what cats do but how they *are* that is so impactful. It is their "attentiveness," she notes, that can teach us the most about practicing magic.

"Cats are delicate, fierce, they pay attention and they notice," she says. "They ride energy. . . . This is all without words, often without sound. Being with creatures who speak differently than we do is crucial; it teaches noticing, it teaches energetic literacy. No diviner is any good without these skills."

Hello Kitty
and the Cult of Cute

Hello Kitty's house appears to be crafted entirely out of confectioners' sugar. White cloud-shaped moldings peek out from the eaves. Baby-pink wrought iron twists into hearts on the balcony. Pastel-blue light beams from the windows. Sandwiched between two candy cane pillars, the front door is outfitted with stained-glass roses. A crowd breathless with excitement gathers in a line outside, waiting to enter her life-size abode. There are schoolgirls in uniform, Gothic Lolitas decked out in funereal fashions, and office ladies buttoned up in business wear.

They all bear the mark of the beast.

Like this motley crew, I have long been enamored with the cartoon superstar and made a six-thousand-mile pilgrimage to Tokyo's Sanrio Puroland (a theme park for Sanrio characters) to submerge myself in all things Kitty. On the way from Shinjuku

Station to the Tama City stop, I took a subway train decorated with her beckoning paw. Pops of pink on the maps and signs leading up to Puroland marked my descent into HK territory. There was no turning back.

Inside Hello Kitty's house, everything is the shape of her face: the shelves, the old-fashioned wood-burning stove, the television—they all have cat ears. Everything morphs to mirror her silhouette. It's an apt metaphor for what has happened over the past forty years. Her adorable visage hasn't changed; the world has changed to fit her. Two pointed ears, no mouth, and a big, flouncy bow: Hello Kitty has become an unblinking icon of feminine cuteness.

Hello Kitty (full name: Kitty White) is five apples tall, in third grade, and lives in the suburbs of London with her parents and twin sister Mimmy. Despite appearances, she is a girl, and *not* a cat, according to Sanrio. Kitty sprang, fully formed, Athena-like, from the mind of Yuko Shimizu back in 1974. An affinity for felines and an assignment to create new characters for Sanrio inspired her to design the cartoon.

"I've always loved animals since childhood," Shimizu tells me during an interview at New York City's Japan Society. "My father bought me a white cat on my third birthday. I think that was the origin of inspiration."

Initially, Hello Kitty was for kids only. She was depicted in the same pose—seated sideways with head facing forward—and appeared on lunch boxes and coin purses and stationery in primary colors. By the late 1970s and into the '80s, Sanrio began marketing HK to adults, and her merchandise, not to mention her color palette and poses, expanded exponentially. By the 2000s, her core customers were women ages eighteen to forty.

Today, Hello Kitty remains a multibillion-dollar phenomenon. She has been the face of haute couture fashion shows and fine art exhibitions. There are Hello Kitty housewares, Hello Kitty shoes and clothing, Hello Kitty luxury goods, Hello Kitty vehicles, and even Hello Kitty vibrators.

When asked why she thinks the character has had such staying power, Shimizu simply says "the cuteness of the design."

Although cute is a universal phenomenon, you can't talk about cute without talking about Japanese visual culture. The embryonic stages of what we now know as cute (or, in Japanese, *kawaii*) trace back to Edo period (1603–1868) paintings and prints. (Utagawa Kuniyoshi's prints of cats cavorting in kimonos or parodying the fifty-three stations on the Tōkaidō Road come to mind.) By the 1970s, the cute explosion reignited in Japan and began to spread.

"The importance of Japanese *kawaii* in the genealogy of cute aesthetics gives the lie to the taken-for-granted dominance of 'Western' cultures," the authors of *The Aesthetics and Affects of Cuteness* explain. Although the experience of cuteness may be universal and does vary according to cultural context, there is only one country that holds the patent.

But what *is* cute? Cuteness may seem indefinably elusive, but it does have a distinctive place in our bleeding hearts. Joshua Paul Dale offers a comprehensive definition in his article "The Appeal of the Cute Object." He writes:

> *Cuteness occupies both the aesthetic and affective realms. As an affect, cuteness comprises a set of visual and/or behavioral characteristics capable of triggering a physical and emotional response in the body of the subject: what we may term the "Aww factor." As an aesthetic category, this response is manipulated for a variety of purposes: commercial to be sure, but also artistic and self-expressive.*

Babies are one model for human perceptions of cuteness. Their wide eyes, chubby cheeks, and general roundness and stubbiness provoke a reaction that can inspire both delight and caretaking. However, viewing anything cute can trigger a rush of dopamine. The so-called "Aww factor" you experience when being awash in cuteness elicits parental and childlike feelings that run the gamut from play to care, according to cute scholars.

Either way, reactions to cuteness do help when you're trying to sell a product. The second part of Dale's definition—cuteness as an aesthetic category—is something the creators of Hello Kitty have mined to great commercial success. However, there's also the "artistic and self-expressive" side Dale mentions. How do we express our own identities through the lens of cuteness and cute products? This question is one that gender theorists have spent some time exploring.

Because of her widespread appeal to both adult women and young girls, Hello Kitty is an apt symbol to explore ideals of "feminine cuteness." At first glance, she has feline attributes in both name and aesthetic. Given the pervasive coding of cats as feminine, Hello Kitty's proximity to *felininity* is an important choice. However, she is not just a cat, but an anthropomorphized cat—a kind of aspirational human-cat hybrid that is arguably easier to identify with than a full feline. Unlike a real cat, HK can join you wherever you go. (These days, Kitty has an actual pet cat that is far more catlike than her, named Charmmy Kitty.)

Another characteristic of Kitty is the design of her face and body. Wide eyes, big round head, and chubby appendages all mimic a human baby's features. Biological essentialists might say these features remind female consumers of the future children they wish to have, making HK all the more appealing to them. In that sense, she is a kind of cat-baby doll. Then again, there is the simpler explanation that Hello Kitty's appearance merely uses cuteness to move more product.

Because she has no mouth, Kitty must transmit all her feelings through her eyes. According to Sanrio, her mouthlessness is supposed to inspire you to imbue HK with your own thoughts and feelings. But many a cultural commentator has had plenty to say about the implications of this design choice.

In the catalog for Japan Society Gallery's 2011 exhibition of young, subversive Japanese artists, "Bye Bye Kitty!!!" curator David Elliott suggests that the mouthless cat cartoon has been detrimental to views about Japanese aesthetics and people. "There is no room for Kitty's blankness here," he notes, introducing art by up-and-comers—including multiple feminist artists—who are vocal about using their work to challenge traditional gender roles.

Anthropologist Christine Yano also references Hello Kitty's blankness—or, rather, her "carefully constructed design of aestheticized, feminized blankness." In *Pink Globalization: Hello Kitty's Trek across the Pacific*, she cites a variety of perspectives on Hello Kitty's lack of mouth. Some fans she interviewed didn't notice or thought it was cute, but others said a lack of mouth can't be a "mere stylistic convention" and is instead something far more horrifying.

"Given a Euro-American political emphasis on speech as the assertion of individual rights, literally not having the means to voice one's opinion or defend one's position may be interpreted as powerlessness," Yano writes. She also includes interviews with performance artists, feminists, and sex workers who aim to give Hello Kitty (and, by extension, Japanese and/or Asian sex workers, Asian women, and women in general) a voice through their art and activism.

By all accounts, Hello Kitty is the opposite of the feral feminine. She is, instead, the height of domestication. However, there are moments when she—and her beloved fans—transcend her safe, clean, and cute aesthetic. The iconography of Hello Kitty is overwhelmingly youthful and sweet, but she has also donned more daring accoutrements that belie her innocence.

Take, for example, the Empress of the Underworld figurine designed by Frank Kozik and produced by Sanrio and Kidrobot in 2009. Based on a painting called *Hekate Kitty* named after the Greek goddess of witchcraft and the underworld, Kitty's face is flushed into a scarlet rage. She holds a pitchfork in one hand and throws devil horns in the other—which isn't too off-brand for someone born on the Day of the Dead. Pentagrams pepper her neon-green outfit. A small spider is included in the package. The Empress of the Underworld is not here for your shit.

On my own mission to uncover Hello Kitty's dark side, I once found a collection of faux barbed-wire jewelry on the goth floor of the Marui shopping mall in Tokyo's Shinjuku district. Little pieces of plastic imitating shards of glass hung like charms from the metal twists. They were printed with pictures of Kitty's face, which was covered in bandages and flecks of blood as if she had just stepped away from a brutal catfight.

And then there's the not-so-dark but certainly not kid-approved Hello Kitty vibrator (marketed by Sanrio as a back massager) that once got me hassled by airport security in Berlin. The *New York Times* covered the popularity of this misappropriated product in a 2007 piece: "Is Hello Kitty Turning Feral?" in which Sanrio reps doubled down on its purpose to "ease aching shoulder muscles."

These "alternative" products push the boundaries of what feminine cuteness is, but there is a limit to how subversive an accessory made by a multibillion-dollar company can be. That said, such objects still have cathartic uses.

Many Hello Kitty lovers—women in particular—view the mouthless cat not just as a product to be acquired and collected, but as a kind of magical charm. Her presence acts as a calming agent, a reminder of the innocence of youth and the sweetness of life unencumbered by oppressive gender roles and the responsibilities of adulthood. To those like Amanda McCarty, creative professional and curator of the *kawaii* blog *Hooray It's Dream Day*, Hello Kitty has been a literal lifesaver.

"I had cancer as a small child, which meant I spent a lot of time in the hospital until about third grade," McCarty explains. "I think people started giving me these Hello Kitty gifts because they knew I loved cats, but over time, the actual Hello Kitty-ness of them became meaningful to me. They were a small taste of sweetness in days that were otherwise filled with pain and sickness. Soon Hello Kitty began to feel like a magical talisman that gave me strength. Seeing something cute and happy reminded me that there was going to be a life outside of this hospital and if I survived, I could be a part of it."

After McCarty survived cancer and reached adulthood, her love of all things Hello Kitty continued—albeit somewhat under the radar. "As a young adult, I felt a little embarrassed about my love of HK," she admits. "So I would just carry a key chain or pencil case—something low key that wouldn't prevent others from taking me seriously as an intellectual, while still allowing me to draw on that precious HK strength."

In a variety of traditions, talismans serve to draw blessings and benefits while protecting witches, magicians, and everyday folk from the pitfalls of hexes, curses, evil, and misfortune. These objects range from jewelry and charms to crystals and other natural objects and can be inscribed with prayers or spells or sigils—but there are no definitive rules about what a talisman looks like.

Protective talismans against the evil eye, for example, are prevalent in many cultures, but one of the most recognizable is the Turkish *nazar*, which consists of concentric circles of glass in shades of blue, white, and black, mimicking the shape of an eye. Other beliefs distinguish protective charms, sometimes called amulets, from talismans, which are intended for manifestation and are charged with an intention through moonlight, spellwork, or one's own will. The nineteenth-century occultists in the Hermetic Order of the Golden Dawn defined the talisman in this way, as "a magical figure charged with the Force which it is intended to represent."

Israel Regardie cites the Golden Dawn's instructions for creating these powerful charms in *How to Make and Use Talismans*: "In the construction of a Talisman, care should be taken to make it, as far as is possible, so to represent the universal Forces that it should be in exact harmony with those you wish to attract, and the more exact the symbolism, the easier it is to attract the Force."

By hijacking the "Aww factor," Hello Kitty's ascent into talismanic territory has indeed been awesome. A figure fixed in a state of childlike wonder who often appears in the color of self-love—pink—this small white cat has been charming devotees for decades.

Amanda McCarty now carries Kitty's magic in a new way. When she turned forty, she finally got inked with a Hello Kitty tattoo, sealing her talisman's power in blood. This drew criticism from coworkers and boyfriends and, in her words, "people who see Hello Kitty (and anything *kawaii*) as weak or inappropriate for adults." But it also brought her a romantic partner down for the *kawaii* ride and an even closer relationship with the *kawaii* community.

"*Kawaii* (including Hello Kitty) is a cultural revolution started by girls and women," McCarty emphasizes. "That's so feminist and badass! There is also this sense of female community at the heart of Hello Kitty." And when McCarty attended Hello Kitty Con in Los Angeles in 2014, she got in touch with fellow HK fans in emotional new ways.

"Hello Kitty fills me with a sense of joy that gives me strength to get through tough days," McCarty muses. "However, if I'm super immersed in Hello Kitty-ness, I will literally cry! It's too much for me! I experienced this for the first time at Hello Kitty Con. I was watching an incredibly cheesy song-and-dance performance featuring Hello Kitty surrounded by a group of dancers. It was terrible! The kind of thing I would normally laugh at! But I looked around at all of the happy faces around me and I just started crying."

Group rituals of ecstatic revelry like the one McCarty describes are hardly different from those performed hundreds—sometimes thousands—of years ago in cults dedicated to deities like Bastet, Diana, and Hekate. Contemporary connotations of "cult" may be laden with menace and coercion, but the original association of the term is with devotion.

For those who engage with Hello Kitty knowing full well she's a marketing ploy and capitalist gimmick and for those who are blissfully ignorant of it all, the love, catharsis, healing, and joy that Hello Kitty devotees engage in are genuine. Such is the enduring magic of a single cute cat.

Cat's Call

Now that we're privy to the magic of cats and why humans of the past and present have been called by them, it's worth it to pause and take stock of the cat's call itself. Music to a pet owner's ears, feline vocalizations are so iconic that even the phrase "the cat's meow" is synonymous with reaching the height of excellence.

"Do not ignore your cat when she meows," commands the ASPCA on its website. And how could you? Some might be able to tear themselves away from the insistent cries that follow them from room to room, but it's not designed to be so easy. Purring, trilling, yelping, yowling, mewling, growing: the sounds of Felis catus are infinite and often crafted to pour honey into human ears.

During kittenhood, cats plead with their mothers for food or warmth through their meows. Come adulthood, cats cut out this kind of vocalizing and rely on a variety of visual and scent-based cues along with the occasional yowl (for sex) and growl (for fights).

After millennia of living among people, however, felines have found their own ways to get our attention.

Most adult cats know that the mouthfeel of meow fits best to communicate with humans and have thus engineered their meowing and purring to target our emotions and get us to do their bidding. Research has demonstrated that the frequencies of a cat's cry and a human baby's are in the same range of 300–600 Hz, and felines have hijacked the innate human response to protect our young for interspecies care.

"In the domestic cat, many signals given when interacting with humans seem to originate from the period of dependency on the mother," behavioral ecologist Karen McComb explains in a study published in *Current Biology*. Just as humans may use baby talk to speak to the adored felines in their charge, cats, too, revert to the cries of their youth when they attempt to communicate. But when cats really want results, they embed their meows into a purr.

McComb's study found that this so-called "solicitation purr" was more likely to be judged by human participants as "more urgent and less pleasant," which often did the trick of getting their owners' attention.

"While solicitation purrs may not have the obvious urgency of the wails of hungry/distressed human infants, their particular acoustic characteristics are likely to make them very difficult to ignore," the study concludes. Few animals on earth have deigned to manipulate their behavior to work us in such a way.

When humans vocalize about cats, however, we are also likely to attract attention. Feline-adjacent language tumbles off the tongue in catlike ways. Lips coil into a pout and voice boxes rumble to "purr." Consonants get nine lives with a "hiss." Tongues brush up lightly against teeth to "slink." This is sensuous language to describe a most sensuous animal. And when the subject of eroticized femininity and feral flesh arises, that language is feline-adjacent, too.

The Oxford English Dictionary traces *cat* as a "term of contempt for a human being," particularly "a spiteful or backbiting woman," to c. 1225. *Catty*, meaning "devious and spiteful," dates to 1886 and has similar implications and gendering as the early usage of cat. In the same vein, *catfight* has been a term for a physical altercation between women since the nineteenth century. The *OED* cites an 1854 account by B.G. Ferris about Mormons in Utah building separate houses for their many wives so they could "keep the women . . . as much as possible, apart, and prevent those terrible cat-fights which sometimes occur, with all the accompaniments of . . . torn caps, and broken broom-sticks." Jealousy over sharing scarce male resources—and a mocking attitude toward women's emotions—was the first context for human female catfights and has kept that context ever since.

Cat also has a strong sexual connotation and was used as slang for a sex worker as early as c. 1401. *To cat around*, however, meaning to have as many sexual partners as you please, is far more ambiguous with dates. (With all this fuzzy feline language, it's not a stretch that heavy petting came to mean hard-core make outs by the 1950s.)

The crown jewel in the lexicon of cats, however, is *pussy*. Pussycats, pussy hats, and pussy hounds: the power of *pussy* is pervasive. As a slur, it is synonymous with weakness. As a noun, it is a vaginal signifier. (Some gay men, trans women, and gender nonconforming folks also use it to describe their pleasure parts, too.) Although etymologists confirm that the origin of *pussy* in reference to vaginas and vulvas isn't definitive, plenty of linguistic trails can be traced through the centuries. Spoken language does have an ephemeral quality, predating written records by decades, so we'll never know exactly when *pussy* first passed a pair of lips.

The use of *puss* to refer to a cat as well as a girl, woman—or feminine man—can be found in written form as early as the early 1500s. In Middle Low German, *pūse* referred to both a woman and a cat, and in Dutch *poes* did as well, which might be the origin of the word in English. Still, *puss* means "pouch" or "purse" in Old Norse, so other etymologists suggest there is no cat connection at all.

Although *pussy* as slang for pudenda supposedly only dates back to 1879, it is likely far, far older. In an episode of *Lexicon Valley*, a podcast that explores the twisting turns of linguistics, the hosts first find *pussy* in its contemporary usage in a bawdy ballad by Thomas D'Urfey. The 1707 song "Puss in a Corner" recounts the plight of an eighteen-year-old woman who is frustrated by her sixty-year-old husband. When the husband asks her why she pouts, she responds: "But only you starve my Cat."

The balladeer elaborates: "A pretty young Kitty, She had that could Purr; 'Twas gamesome and handsome, And had a rare Fur; And straight-up I took it, and offer'd to stroake it; In hopes I should make it kind."

The double entendres continue, and the young girl asks her husband to fetch John, who has been known to solve her "problem" in the past. (John was also a slang term for penis.) "As felt as my Feet, Could convey me I sped, to Johnny who many times Pussey had fed." Lo and behold, the magnanimous gentleman shows up at her beck and call. The surrogate lover is kind enough to satisfy her kitty's cravings, and so the couple's May-December romance marches on.

Ever since dirty limericks like these were shared across tavern tables, *pussy* has been slang for the vulva and/or vagina, and cats have invoked vaginas, too. You'll find this represented visually on branding for menstruation products (when you order a pair of Thinx period panties, confirmation emails include a little illustrated black cat); on book covers about female sexuality (Meika Hollender's *Get on Top: Of Your Pleasure, Sexuality & Wellness: A Vagina Revolution* has a furry feline face staring out); and on the most ubiquitous pink hat feminist activists have ever worn. Cunning linguists and comedians alike have made it the centerpiece of their jokes, and pussy havers and lovers have managed at times to reclaim the word from patriarchal clutches, too.

Pussy Hats and Homocats

"Pussy Grabs Back"

"Cats Against Cat Calls"

"The Future Is Feline"

Cat-centric messaging has overtaken feminist action. Emblazoned on placards, T-shirts, and banners, cat puns and cat imagery have been clawing their way into gender politics since the turn of the twentieth century.

In the early 1900s, when suffragists were making strides toward voting rights for women, cats were part of the pushback. On one infamous British postcard, an angry black kitten, jaws open in a hiss or rousing meow, sits petulantly above the words "I want my vote!" A similar postcard features a gray cat in an oversize hat adorned with feathers and a small bird. The cat's shawl is held together with a "Votes for Women" button, and beneath its paws reads: "We Demand the Vote."

Satirical postcards like these were disseminated by those opposed to the cataclysmic cultural shift suffragists were advocating for. "We don't care if we never have a vote," reads another postcard featuring two cats who stare out solemnly. Opponents of equal rights cast women as silly, intellectually inferior, and, like domestic cats, only meant to be kept. Cat imagery like this positioned women as animals, a species distinct from men, and undeserving of their same rights. Men were men, and women? They were cats.

When the cat's sister in suffering—the witch—was being reclaimed as an archetype for feminist action, the cat came with her. In 1968, guerrilla theater group W.I.T.C.H. (Women's International Terrorist Conspiracy from Hell) used the aesthetics of the wicked woman cribbed from Hollywood film and European folklore to critique patriarchal systems of power. They staged protests in the form of mock hexes and conjured up clever slogans all while dressed in witchy garb.

"Whatever is repressive, solely male-oriented, greedy, puritanical, authoritarian—those are your targets," reads a mission statement from the founding New York chapter. "Your weapons are theater, satire, explosions, magic, herbs, music, costumes, cameras, masks, chants . . . brooms, guns . . . cats"—the list goes on. Although cats were never used as actual weapons, the feline had firmly fallen in with the feminist camp.

Forty-eight years later, feminist-cat messaging reached peak popularity.

Beloved, belittled, cute, and contested, the pussy hat came to prominence as the symbol of a new wave of feminist resistance after Trump won the 2016 election. At the time, two Los Angeles–based professionals, artist and architect Jayna Zweiman and screenwriter Krista Suh, had recently taken up crocheting. Suh was venturing to the Women's March in Washington, DC, the day after Trump's inauguration, and Zweiman could not attend any of the marches due to an injury. They both concocted the idea of creating a visual representation of solidarity that could sweep the streets and the screens of folks in favor of women's rights.

According to the Pussyhat Project, owner of the Little Knittery Kat Coyne designed the pussy hat to be simple enough so that even beginning knitters could participate. The now-trademarked pussy hat was born out of frustration and solidarity with those opposed to Donald Trump's sexist and antichoice views, along with his egregious recorded statement on *Entertainment Tonight* about his penchant for grabbing women "by the pussy" without their consent.

All it took was a bit of social media magic and the fashion statement took off.

The pussy hat made it onto the heads of thousands of marchers, and it made headlines too. The cover of *Time* for the February 6, 2017, issue features a single pink pussy hat, ears erect and hopeful, next to the headline: "The Resistance Rises: How a March Becomes a Movement." The cover of *The New Yorker* released on the same date also featured a pussy hat, this time worn by a cocoa-skinned Rosie the Riveter. But despite the pussy hat's popularity, it was not without its vocal critics.

Many Republicans criticized those wearing pussy hats for being childish, silly, or sore losers. The men who wore them in solidarity were particularly mocked for engaging in this supposedly effeminate act. (Pink + cats = the height of femininity, you see.) Comedian Sacha Baron Cohen even created a character skewering white male liberals whose signature look includes a pussy hat. In his show *Who Is America?*, the fictional Dr. Nira Cain-N'Degeocello is the author of *Masculinity and Other Hate Crimes* and is a self-flagellating caricature of a male feminist.

Critics of the pussy hat were not only on the right, however. Some thought the symbol was benign, indicative of a feminism that has gone soft, consumerist, and ineffective. Feminist anarchists could be spotted wearing the slogan "put down the pussy hat / pick up a baseball bat." Other queer and transgender folks and their allies balked at the idea that fighting for gender equality must be associated with any anatomical feature, especially because those who identify as women do not all have "pussies" in the first place. And many leftists and Democrats of color saw the pussy hat as a symbol of the white feminism that Hillary Clinton embodied, where she declared "women's rights are human rights" one moment and then called black children "superpredators" the next.

When a pussy hat was photographed on a statue of Harriet Tubman in New York City in 2018, Doreen St. Félix unpacked a variety of these tense issues in a piece for *The New Yorker*. She discussed the "white-feminist appropriation of black intellectual labor" and why the hat atop a renowned black freedom fighter might not be the best fit—to say the least.

"The pussyhat, too, has been ridiculed: for its origin in a repellent Trump slur, for its possible exclusion of transgender women, for its flippant embrace of the racial connotations of pink. The hat does not belong on Tubman," St. Félix writes. "Or, depending on who's looking, it does."

This ambivalence has defined the discourse surrounding the pussy hat. But regardless of where one falls on the spectrum of pussy hat appreciation, it does not change how much cultural weight has been given to donning two pink cat ears.

Taking on cat characteristics has political impact. It is a signifier of femininity and womanhood, but more than that, it can also signal resistance against obedience to authority. The cat, after all, still retains much of its wild nature.

Since 2010, Brooklyn-based artist J. Morrison has been fusing feline imagery and queer politics in bright, bold colors and wearable prints. "Homocats Fight Phobias" reads one of his famous designs beneath a British shorthair staring daggers. "Kitten Revolution" exclaims another print, as two muscle-bound male bodies with cat heads flex beneath. "Kill Guns" a banner implores in front of a snarling feline. Undeniably appealing yet unsettling, these aesthetic and ideological juxtapositions invite you to come for the cute and stay for the coup.

"Being an avid cat lover and a political artist, I wanted to combine the popularity of the feline with social commentary," Morrison explains. "I was inspired by early cat memes such as *I Can Has Cheezburger* and *LOLcats*, but I wanted to insert some activism into my images."

Morrison's first drawing in the series features two black cats and two white ones turning their heads to stare back at us, with "We Are Tired of Homophobia" written in cursive beneath. "It's unfortunately still relevant eight years later," Morrison adds. "I've always considered the HOMOCATS mission statement to be 'to fight phobias, propose equal rights, combat cultural stereotypes, challenge social norms, and now, to resist Trump.'"

As the project gained visibility and popularity, cats became Morrison's permanent canvas. "Cats are one of the most popular social media phenomena, and HOMOCATS play off that trend to subvert their message," Morrison says. "They have allowed me the freedom to reach the general public via the Internet, Instagram, and art fairs and exhibitions. I love felines for their independence, smarts, and unique sensibilities."

Inspired by his long-standing love of felines, Morrison's own cats have played a part in his political art. "My *Kittens Against Trump* series was inspired by my Siamese cat Charley," Morrison says. "Using the filter of the HOMOCATS, I created it shortly after the election out of sheer desperation. I loved the wide-eyed look of shock and horror that Siamese often have, and their ability to be very vocal and talk a lot. If he was still with us, I know he would have a lot to say on the matter!"

Like the pussy hat, the HOMOCATS have become an aesthetic offshoot of the resistance. As the Trump administration continues to attack the rights of queer and trans folks, women, people of color, and immigrants, cat iconography is front and center.

"Not surprisingly, my *Kittens Against Trump* work has been the most popular but has also allowed for more opposing views in response," Morrison notes. "I feel our current political climate has opened the door for more accepted homophobia, bigotry, and racism in society. Personally, I feel the HOMOCATS represent the crux of the problem here in the US: In the aftermath of the 2016 election, can we as a society honestly say we are fully ready to accept diversity? For instance, everyone loves cats, but will everyone accept the HOMOCATS as a minority?"

What makes Morrison's art so discomfiting are provocations like these, which force viewers to push past the warm fuzzies that a cute face conjures and take a political position. The antithesis of cat videos and cat memes, which millions indulge in mindlessly, HOMOCATS beckons us to reject apathy—radicalize even—or, at the very least, think. In the summer of 2018, Morrison invited friends and colleagues to wear his art in a part-march, part-birthday party along the High Line, an elevated park in New York City. On a balmy night in August, attendees were each given one of his shirts: a shocking pink tank with a bright blue cat's face emblazoned across it. We were then instructed to put it on and queue up single file. As we walked, tourists with cameras taking in views of the Hudson River and locals hanging out on benches getting stoned stared and chuckled—or shouted out to the group about their own love of cats.

Taking my place in the midst of the line that snaked through the throng of sightseers, I started talking to Morrison's friends about cats and how they play such a pivotal role in so many of our lives. One man shared the heartbreaking story about the death of his cat. Another told me that back when he had three cats, his gay male friends chastised him and said he'd never get a boyfriend because of it. They implored him not to mention a whisker of his menagerie on his Grindr profile. The man laughed and said that if he were to invite any of his hookups over, they would see the cats anyway, so why would it matter?

The maligned "cat lady" designation still waits in the wings, a threat to any person, gay or straight, male or female, who dares to be single and own cats.

A few weeks after the birthday march, I asked Morrison about the association of cats with femininity and what that might mean for his work. He does, after all, sell a pair of briefs in his online store that read "MASC 4 CAT" and are shown filled out with a ripe bulge.

"The HOMOCATS intend to question cultural norms and expectations," he explains. "I thought it was an interesting parallel combining the perception that cats are more feminine creatures, along with the stereotypes of gay men being feminine, as well as the notion that being gay and/or feminine is still viewed as less than by the general public."

With his cheeky MASC 4 CAT designs, Morrison flips the script on this conversation.

"The MASC 4 CAT (taken from the Masculine for Masculine phrase) was created as a humorous commentary about questioning subdivision even in smaller communities," he says.

"Masc 4 Masc" became a contentiously popular phrase on the hookup app Grindr in the past decade, denoting a masculine man in search of another masculine man—no exceptions. It was roundly criticized by many inside and outside the gay and queer communities who saw it as a reflection of exclusionary perspectives that not only stigmatize trans women and folks on the feminine spectrum, but reflect the same kind of sexism that feminism fights against the world over. When such a serious issue is couched in cat imagery, however, it simultaneously softens it while calling into relief its absurdity.

Morrison's work makes many serious political issues more palatable, but at the same time, they are even harder to ignore. Such is the power of HOMOCATS. "In my experience with the general public throughout the States, I do honestly feel people want to respond and get involved, but many are unable or just don't know how," Morrison affirms. "It is my hope that radical felines can help inspire and bring about social change."

Tomcats and Feline Casanovas

The affiliation between the feline and the feminine is undeniable, but that doesn't mean there isn't room for masculinity in the equation. So when are cats male, and when are men cats?

Men are cats when they're fierce, superhuman warriors like Marvel's Black Panther or ancient Aztec jaguar knights. Men are cats when they're crotch-thrusting live wires, out "tomcatting"—i.e., pursuing as many partners as they can seduce simultaneously. Men are cats when they're Rum Tum Tugger: perverse, preening, and independent, or when they're feline Casanovas from "Stray Cat Strut." Tapping into sexual abandon, flying in the face of decorum, taking on primal power: that's when men are cats.

But when are cats men? Male cats are often still associated with human women, but there are critical moments when cats are distinctly "men," like the satanic feline with the erect tail in *Vox in Rama*; Behemoth, the vodka-downing jokester in Mikhail

Bulgakov's *The Master and Margarita*; or Salem from the original TV show *Sabrina the Teenage Witch*, a man forced to endure a feline form for trying to take over the world—who sometimes impersonates a woman in a chat room for attention. Tapping into sexual abandon, flying in the face of decorum, taking on primal power: that's when cats are men.

Men are cats when they are hypermasculine, hot and bothered, chasing tail. But men are also cats when they're eschewing heterosexual norms.

Back in the medieval era, when the word *puss* became a term for a woman, it was also used to refer to a gay or feminine man. Queerness in men has long been associated with femininity, so much of the same cat-adjacent language for women has also been slapped onto gay men. And because cats have been coded as feminine for so long, some men hell-bent on proving their heterosexual masculinity have gone to great lengths to avoid being perceived as cat lovers.

In the early twentieth century, when photography was a new medium, a single shot could speak volumes about how you would like to be portrayed. In *The Photographed Cat*, authors Arnold Arluke and Lauren Rolfe analyze how people were pictured with their pets between 1900 and 1940. What they found was that men were photographed being affectionate with a variety of animals, but far less with cats. Whereas women would cradle cats and treat them as secondary (or primary) children, men eschewed such intimacy, presumably because of the association of cats with women, femininity, and the soft embrace of motherhood.

"When pictured with cats, men a century ago appeared to carefully avoid poses that might suggest intimacy," the authors write. "The most common way that photographs captured male displays of role distance was by directing their gaze toward the viewer rather than toward the cat subject and by not using their hands to touch or hold the cat, unless the touch was to impose control rather than express affection."

One image included in the text of a craggy, mustachioed gentleman is quite revealing. He stares gruffly at the camera, one hand curled into a light fist as the other hangs at his side. A cat perches on his shoulder, but his pose and demeanor suggest he'd be standing that way whether the cat was there or not.

There is no way to know whether such behaviors in front of the camera reflected this man's true feelings or if he was staging this lack of feline affection for the photographer or those who might see the finished photo. Whatever his intentions, this documented trend of avoidant behavior demonstrates how strongly cats were—and still are—thought to be "women's animals."

This association continues to play out in curious ways.

Take, for example, the contemporary romantic advice book designed for heterosexual men, *The Feline Mystique: A Man's Guide to Living with Cats (and/or Women)*, which has a parallel title for heterosexual women in *All Men ARE Dogs: YOU Are the Dog Trainer*.

Or the fact that in the BDSM community, kitten play is dominated by women, but puppy play is dominated by men. Or that an exclamation of sensual appreciation for a feminine person is "Meow!" while for a masculine person it's "Woof!" These associations are so well-worn they're worthy of parody.

Not only are men dogs, as the misandrous phrase goes, but "dogs are men"—at least according to two female cats in Bruce Eric Kaplan's 2018 New Yorker cartoon. Sitting face-to-face in front of a sofa, two stony-faced cats, deep in conversation, express their deep disapproval for dogs by flipping the script on this common gendered narrative in a single frame.

It's funny because it's true! Or is it funny because it's become a cliché?

Many still hold fast to the cats=pussy and dogs=bone(r)s designation, but there is also a more expansive view on the matter taking hold as gender roles and gender expressions shake loose from their foundations.

With the proliferation of articles like "All hail the rise of cat men, an antidote to toxic masculinity" (ABC); "10 Reasons to Date a Man Who Owns a Cat, because It Actually Makes Him 10 Times More Dateable" (Bustle); and "'Cat men' are the answer to online toxic masculinity" (Metro), perhaps the association between cats and femininity is finally lessening? Or perhaps this "new" kind of masculinity is so appealing to certain women because of its proximity to or mimicry of certain prized feminine attributes?

Whatever the case may be, as some seek to redefine masculinity, cats have, oddly enough, become part of the process.

CatCon—the world's largest cat convention—produced a popular panel in 2017 and 2018 called "Men and Cats: A Love Story." Featuring some of the biggest names in celebrity cats and cat care, it became a place for the community's "favorite Cat Daddies" to discuss "the special felines in their lives."

During the inaugural panel, moderator (and host of podcast *My Favorite Murder*) Georgia Hardstark began by offering an overview of the stigma against cat-loving men.

"Kinda like the phrase crazy cat lady, men have also gotten a bad rap when it comes to showcasing their love for our kitty friends," said Hardstark. "But, luckily, now, it seems like that attitude is shifting, and it's ok to be a cat man, right?" She paused and the audience returned a rousing cheer.

As Arluke and Rolfe point out in *The Photographed Cat*, our association of dogs with men and cats with women may now be "normative," but it was in fact "built into our culture as a taken-for-granted preference, with sanctions to ensure widespread conformity."

Now that these sanctions are slowly being lifted, the future is open for postgender cat appreciation to flourish. But in the meantime, we can still appreciate these eight unsung male cats and cat-loving men.

Mogg

Cat, stoner, and lover of Megg, a green-skinned human witch in Simon Hanselmann's graphic novel series *Megahex*. Mogg often wonders if he's too small for adequate action, but Megg affirms that he's just right for their interspecies love.

MC Skat Kat

Sunglasses and sneaker–wearing cat rapper and cartoon boyfriend of recording artist Paula Abdul. In Abdul's 1988 music video for "Opposites Attract," we learn that while she takes things serious, he takes 'em light. (And she goes to bed early and he parties all night.)

Björk's Feline S.O.

Unnamed controlling partner cat of Björk. In the Icelandic songstress's 2004 music video for "Triumph of the Heart," we are privy to the trying aspects of a cat-woman romance. The cat hangs out at home in his undershirt, while Björk runs off to party with friends—but always returns to the paws of her feline boy toy.

Gloria Estefan's Cat-Men

Unnamed *catanovas* out on the town. In an alternate version of Gloria Estefan's 1985 video for "Bad Boys," she ditches her human date to hang with guys dressed as if they came straight out of a production of the musical *Cats*. These cat-men read "Playcat" magazine, get drunk in public, and take Gloria for a spin in their catmobile.

Freddie Mercury

Inimitable singer of Queen, great lover of cats. He would literally ring up his pets while on tour and ask his human assistants to hold the phone up to their ears. He dedicated his first solo album to his cat Jerry, "also Tom, Oscar and Tiffany, and all the cat lovers across the universe—screw everybody else!" Mercury wrote a sultry song about his favorite pussy, Delilah, on Queen's final album, *Innuendo*.

Abraham Lincoln

Sixteenth president of the United States and cat obsessive who kept multiple pets at the White House. He once stopped to save three orphaned kittens during a trip to Virginia in the waning days of the Civil War. Treasury official Maunsell B. Field wrote of Lincoln in his memoirs: "Mr. Lincoln possessed extraordinary kindness of heart when his feelings could be reached. He was fond of dumb animals, especially cats. I have seen him fondle one for an hour." When Mary Todd Lincoln was asked about her husband's hobbies, she simply replied, "cats."

Baudelaire

Poet, rapscallion, and feline devotee. The French wordsmith wrote plenty of stanzas about feline mystery, calling cats "partisans of carnal dalliance and science," lauding their "fertile loins" where a "sparkling magic lies."

Mark Twain

Writer and humorist Mark Twain kept dozens of cats at a time, giving them illustrious names of grandeur and import. He also once said: "If man could be crossed with the cat, it would improve man, but it would deteriorate the cat."

Animality and the Mystical Digital

Contemporary conjurers are now harnessing the digital as they are the physical. They're anointing iPhones before writing auspicious emails, swiping through dating apps with the most blessed of intentions, tracking moon cycles and astrological events on retinal displays, and sharing spells and rituals through social channels as communal hexing and healing fly across fiber optics. In the digital realm witches do trend, and magic does dominate many dark corners of the internet, but that's *nothing* compared to cats. The cat may have long been the sorceress's sidekick, but online, the acolyte has become the adept.

Cats aren't just *on* the internet, cats *are* the internet. Although cat content online doesn't outnumber content featuring other animals, it is still the most likely to trend. From Instagram "meowmies" and their star fur babies with multimillion-dollar licensing deals to *LOLcats* and *I Can Has Cheezburger* memes, "cats have been going viral since the Ptolemies ruled the Nile," quips Abigail Tucker in *The Lion in the Living Room*. In fact, cats are so popular in the digital sphere that they have become synonymous with it.

"Cats are the mascots of being online," explains Amanda Hess in a *New York Times* video. "They are the epitome of distracting, useless and comforting. All that the internet is at its best and at its worst." But how is it that cats have come to cast their spell on us in this way?

Our feline overlords have been the subject of countless computations, studies, and think pieces to understand the cause and consequence of this addiction. Cultural anthropologists, journalists, scientists, and sociologists alike have long been trying to suss out why we're so drawn to cute animals like cats and why we spend thousands of hours looking at them on our screens. There is ample evidence that doing so does offer an emotional boost and stress reduction, particularly during the workday, but is there something else?

To cat-loving artist Carolee Schneemann, the popularity of online cat content is "a feminist revolution." In an interview with the *Huffington Post*, Schneemann lauds the fact that our collective attentions have been showered upon an animal that doesn't follow the rules. She views this as a shift "away from the insistence that the only good pet is the responsive, obedient, happy dog."

"The cat, like female sexuality, has always occupied a place of unpredictability, uncontrollability," Schneemann continues. "Something too soft and fuzzy that also has claws. All these ambiguous aspects of cats had for many years been suspect."

In an article for the *M/C Journal*, Radha O'Meara discusses the possible subversive implications of watching cat videos on YouTube. (There are well over two million.) Although many have deemed this time-sucking act devoid of meaning, O'Meara argues that doesn't have to be the case. Because the cats in cat videos do not know they are being watched and are free from self-consciousness, she suggests that viewers can vicariously take on cat subjectivity and experience life without surveillance—or self-surveillance.

"Unselfconsciousness is associated with privacy, intimacy, naivety and, increasingly, with impossibility," she writes. "By allowing us to project onto the experience of their protagonists, cat videos invite us to imagine a world where we are not constantly aware of being watched, of being under surveillance by both human beings and technology. This projection is enabled by discourse, which constructs cats as independent and aloof, a libertarian ideal. . . . Through cat videos, we celebrate the untameable."

This entrée into a seemingly unattainable wild state is similar to how some might view the otherworldly videos and photographs of witchy movers, shakers, and magic makers online. Scroll through any witch-adjacent hashtag on Instagram and you're likely to uncover incense-filled tableaux featuring holographic tarot spreads, dried flower petals, leather-bound grimoires, candles dripping with glitter and wax, and color and fashion magic at work in the curated leather, lace, fringe, or silk wares on the witch sharing her knowledge at the center of it all. Sometimes, there is less production value, and the main event is a body as it was born: bare skin and the bounty of nature in the background—and maybe an animal bone or two.

The subjects of these posts are well aware they're making media to be consumed by countless strangers, but they still offer a peek into a practice that is meant to be embraced for its ephemerality. Such imagery on social media is only the tip of the iceberg that lies beneath. It only hints at years of study, of magical mastery, of shadow work, of digging hands deep in the dirt.

Intuitive spiritual guide, tarot reader, and bruja Valeria Ruelas, also known as @themexicanwitch, is someone who takes pride in sharing her craft online. "Instagram is very important to my business," she tells me. "It has been a great way to reach a much larger audience all over the world that I could honestly never tap into otherwise." But much as she lauds this digital tool and is grateful for the "great community" it offers, Ruelas believes it is vital to practice discretion with what she posts. "I won't share pictures of any spells that I am doing for any clients because that is a *huge* breach of privacy and I pride myself on keeping people's secrets." She also mentions that she doesn't post pictures of client tarot readings or her own personal altar photos or spiritual protection spells. Ruelas has had notable success working with Santa Muerte as of late, but that synergy is something that happens offline, too. "I have started to really feel like an 'occult' practitioner in the past few years because I have a lot of secrets that I want to keep to myself until the greater public is ready to hear them," she reveals.

One look through The Mexican Witch's feed and it's easy to become smitten with Ruelas's vibrant glamour, youthful energy, and incisive yet welcoming witchcraft teachings. However, Ruelas, like other professional witches I have spoken with, knows that the true power and magic of witchcraft and ritual at their most ecstatic and effective cannot really be captured, reproduced, or shared online. It is in these states of communion offline that practitioners aim to embody unself-consciousness—and even transcend the trappings of self and society. Scoff at the #witchesofinstagram all you like, but, like internet cats, many of them can offer access to an untamable world, too.

A historical and mythological mélange has inspired much mystery to be attributed to cats and witchy women, and at the hypnotic heart of all this witch and cat content is the allure of the feral and the feminine. Yes, there are the cats and witches online who will serve no purpose beyond entertainment and visual stimulation, and that's perfectly fine. But that doesn't mean there cannot also be liberating moments for the uninitiated that take place during an endless scroll.

Women and femininity have historically been judged by how pleasing they are to the eye, so what might it mean for women and feminine folks in particular when they observe unselfconscious creatures or practices meant to inspire unselfconsciousness online? Is this act more heightened and impactful for those whose lives have been largely defined culturally, socially, and technologically by being watched? These questions only begin to scratch the surface of how the mystical and the digital may be impacting our lives.

Clawing Her Way Out—
The Politics of Liberation

Celestial, illusory, solitary—the archetypal cat and witch are cut from the same cloth. These shape-shifters have embodied various aspects of the archetypal feminine, their forms and flesh viewed as demonic contagions to be destroyed, erotic enigmas to be dominated, and liberating identities to grasp for agency—or at least great aesthetics. They have both been foils for human desires: malleable bodies on which we project our fears and fantasies. We love them, we hate them, we want to be them, we are them.

There is more at stake, though. The witch and cat aren't simply fashionable icons to emulate and discard once you reach peak #empowerment. And they don't only have to be part of an individual's identity formation, serious and sustaining as that is. The witch and cat are also emblematic of nimbly skirting the dominating forces of patriarchy, capitalism, and neoliberalism. They can be sigils for summoning radical change.

Witches first gained political agency in the era of the suffragists. With the publication of *Woman, Church, and State* in 1893, Matilda Joslyn Gage reframed the early modern European witch hunts as a misogynistic project by the Christian church to cast women and female healers as heretics. Although we now know that the witch hunts were the result of a complex confluence of factors, there is a core truth to Gage's reading. Her view of accused witches would go on to influence feminist narratives about witch persecution and the persecution of women for years to come. The repression of women's rights and the brutalization of women's bodies that occurred during the witch hunts would become righteous fuel for activist groups like W.I.T.C.H. and other feminist covens and spiritual groups that sprang up in the 1970s. Since then, the witch has loomed large in gender politics and social justice movements.

In addition to the gendered symbolism inherent in the European witch hunts, there is economic symbolism to be found, too. Marxist feminist scholar Silvia Federici posits in *Caliban and the Witch: Women, the Body and Primitive Accumulation* that the witch is "the embodiment of a world of female subjects that capitalism had to destroy: the heretic, the healer, the disobedient wife, the woman who dared to live alone, the obeah woman who poisoned the master's food." The exploitation of women and their bodies was necessary to fuel early capitalism, Federici writes, so they could "function as machines for the production of labor."

Taking up the revolutionary aspects of these subjects with new vigor, anti-capitalist and anti-fascist witches of today are harnessing the revolutionary potential of the witch archetype and witchcraft as a tool for social justice. More and more this is manifesting in politically centered covens, the proliferation of healing spells for self and community care, and mass hexes against racist, sexist, and fascist politicians.

The cat has fulfilled a similar role, becoming an aspirational model of defiance.

In the late 1730s, a group of apprentice printers rounded up, tortured, and killed as many cats as they could get their hands on in protest of their harsh working conditions. As Robert Darnton explains in *The Great Cat Massacre*, "cats symbolized witchcraft, sexuality, and domesticity" and their ritual mass murder "was meant simultaneously as a trial, a gang rape, a rebellion of the workers against their boss, and a carnivalesque kind of street theater, which the workers later repeated in the form of pantomime." The Great Cat Massacre had a multiplicity of meanings to those who took part, but class warfare was definitely one of them.

Oddly enough, within two hundred years, the cat would switch sides and become a beacon for Marxism, anarchism, and socialism, signaling uncomfortable truths about bourgeois revolution and bourgeois comforts. Since then, the feline has remained firmly on the left side of the aisle.

In the early 1900s, the formidable labor union Industrial Workers of the World (or IWW) used a ferocious black cat—back arched, ready to attack—as a mascot that packed a visual punch. Labor activist Ralph Chaplin is credited with creating the "sab cat" or "sabo-tabby." During a 1918 trial of IWW leaders, Chaplin noted that the cat is a perfect representation of sabotage. "The idea being to frighten the employer by the mention of the name sabotage, or by putting a black cat somewhere around. You know if you saw a black cat go across your path you would think, if you were superstitious, you are going to have a little bad luck. The idea of sabotage is to use a little black cat on the boss."

Recently, artists Caroline Woolard and Or Zubalsky and scholar Leigh Claire La Berge created a video art project that explores the feline side of Marxism. On the Marx for Cats website, which launched on the 101st anniversary of the Russian Revolution, La Berge speaks about different Marxist topics to a group of cats as they sit enrapt or indifferent, some moving in and out of frame, some playing or starting squabbles.

In a 2018 "Election Day Special" installment, La Berge delves into the idea of the "Katzenjammer" (cat's wail) introduced in Marx's 1851 essay "The Eighteenth Brumaire of Louis Bonaparte." She notes that it's "one of the only texts in which the cat itself becomes a historical figure . . . with revolutionary possibility and revolutionary constriction." And it's very relevant in post-Trump America.

To Marx, the Katzenjammer was a wail or lament that settled upon the citizenry after the French Revolution when true change failed to fully take hold. Marx noted that greed was the culprit, as the bourgeois class "will nullify their own political power to preserve their right for economic exploitation," La Berge elaborates. This ultimately led to a democratically elected leader returning France to a monarchy.

Today, the same thing is ostensibly happening. The rich and powerful remain largely silent in the face of Trump's abuses in exchange for economic benefits. He, like Louis Bonaparte, was elected democratically but has since expressed a distaste for freedoms won through bourgeois revolution (free press, a right to assembly) and an affinity for dictators and fascist policies (Russia, a lifetime presidency).

Marx positioned the cat's wail as both harbinger and cause of hard times to come. But now? Knowing how similar political angling has turned out in the past, it may have a shift in timbre. The cat's call, laden with leftist symbolism in the twenty-first century, could now be heard as a warning against the seductive and destructive aspects of capitalism.

This is how computer scientist Jaron Lanier views the revolutionary feline. To him, the cat represents a subject that eschews Silicon Valley's unfettered neoliberal capitalism. "Cats have done the seemingly impossible," he writes in *10 Arguments for Deleting Your Social Media Accounts Right Now*. "They've integrated themselves into the modern high-tech world without giving themselves up. They are still in charge." Lanier proposes that we all should be like cats, resisting total domination by the technology that has enslaved our habitual minds. To be catlike is to be flexible and clever enough to defy the double bind of life online, while you still might enjoy a cat video or two.

"How can you remain autonomous in a world where you are under constant surveillance and are constantly prodded by algorithms run by some of the richest corporations in history, which have no way of making money except by being paid to manipulate your behavior?" he asks. "How can you be a cat, despite that?"

Lanier's cats are much like Silvia Federici's witches. They represent the kind of subjects who defy economic exploitation. Because the cat and the witch also symbolize a legacy of female power and persecution, they are especially ripe for those fixated on revolution from gender imperialism.

And yet, though the cat and the witch are powerful symbols, they are also rooted in fallible bodies, and there are continually evolving and conflicting ideas about what they stand for. Witches can be revolutionaries, but they can also be stuck in the spiritual realm with no care for earthly consequences—all love and light and no action. Similarly, cats can be icons of the liberating feral feminine, but they can also be solipsistic predators out for themselves alone.

It's also important to remember that neither the women accused of witchcraft in the early modern era nor cats at any point in time likely cared about—or were even cognizant of—political protest. And yet, we can incorporate the ethos of the shape-shifter when it serves us to view witches and cats as emblems of empowerment. It's incredibly appealing in theory, but in practice? Only time will tell how effective these mascots for mobilization—or, at the very least, playful political subversion—will fare.

Tail's End

In myth and magic, art and culture, there's no single fixed point where the feral feminine leads us, but rather a constellation of places and possibilities emerges to sic our curiosities on. Concluding a tale that will continue indefinitely, then, that's always in perpetual motion, shifting shape and evading capture at every turn, is like trying to catch a feral cat. Hold on too tightly, with too much certainty, and it's sure to elude your grasp. Anything too concrete, too emphatic, would be disingenuous—but dramatic? The feline is nothing if not dramatic. In this spirit, there are two possible endings that shine through for me: an experiential one and a theoretical one—a kind of *Black* (Cat) *Mirror* choose your own adventure, if you will.

We'll begin in Las Vegas, surrounded by a bounty of flesh and feline aesthetics at the "Oscars of porn," the AVNs.

I arrived at the Hard Rock Hotel & Casino on a breezy afternoon in January to explore the *Adult Video News* trade show, unsure of what kind of cats I might find inside. Squeezing through a sea of tits and ass and rabid fans taking pictures with their favorite porn stars, I first spotted a booth overflowing with fur and leather cat ears and plush tails—both real and faux. There were some dyed in shades of hot pink and purple and green. Others were more "realistic," with patterns you might find in the wild. Leopard print floggers were nestled near collars that boasted tiny bells—perfect for a beloved pet of any species.

My wanderings continued as I scanned the crowd for more signs of feline life. I noticed some of the cam girls setting up at the MyFreeCams, Brazzers, and ManyVids booths were sporting cat ears. Some ears were fuzzy, some were leather, some were metal filigree. The girls had little else in common—different skin colors, hairstyles, body types, outfits—but they all wore ears. Whether the men eager to interact with them were conscious of the connection doesn't matter. The idea of cats being hypersexual creatures is so deeply ingrained that few would see it as strange if a woman wanting to be more sexually appealing would seek a feline accessory.

Next, I ventured into fetish territory. After being sidetracked by a gentleman who offered to cinch me up in a leather compression cage that was designed to feel like a full-body finger trap, I perused more erotic products. There were leather cat masks, cat-o'-nine-tails, and more folks in cat ears. One booth sold enamel pins of superheroes and pop culture icons depicted as blushing BDSM bois or kinky beauties. Curiously, there was no Catwoman. When I asked the proprietor why, he merely said: "It's too on the nose."

Although rabbits and foxes can be considered sexual icons in their own right, there are no animals more synonymous with sex than those in the felid family. At a place like the AVNs, cat accessories provide this feline energy to consumers through wearable talismans that promise a taste of the erotic abandon central to porn.

Just as I began to believe I had found all the cat-related gems to be had, I got a message from Korby, frontwoman of the band Cougrr, who was filming a promotional segment for her show, *Cougrr TV*. An entertainer and entrepreneur, Korby was at the AVNs interviewing the stars of cougar and MILF porn. For the uninitiated, these older women and "moms I'd like to fuck" are an incredibly popular subgenre within the adult industry. They offer up a combination of maternal instinct and age play by subverting society's preference for nubile bodies in favor of more seasoned flesh. The cougar may be on the other end of the spectrum from the sex kitten, but they both sharpen their claws in the nexus where the feline and feminine meet.

Korby herself began identifying as a cougar once she ended a seven-year-long relationship, turned forty, was diagnosed with and survived breast cancer, experienced a sexual awakening, and began dating younger men—whom she affectionately calls "cubs."

"I discovered that dating younger men in their twenties is truly where it's at," she tells me amid the din of the casino. "There are two things that converged at one time. I felt like I had gotten to the next level of the video game, the secret level, where my body, my orgasms, everything when I'm having sex is so much more pleasurable and enjoyable, and I'm so much more in control. It's like I took a magic pill, but it's just called being in your prime—and they're in their prime, too."

After she regaled me with tales of her sexploits (some of which are chronicled in the Cougrr song "Year of the Cock"), I brought the conversation back to cats. Why are they called cougars, I wondered? Korby admitted that it could be any kind of wildcat, but there is something particularly strong and feminine about a cougar's face.

Unlike a MILF, who can technically be any age, cougars have distinct parameters. "You have to be forty and up, otherwise you can call yourself a puma or a cougar-in-training," Korby instructs. "But it's something you earn. You turn forty. Nobody wants to get older, it's a big birthday, there's a lot of stress associated with it, especially for women. So if you're a single woman and you're forty, it's a way to turn what used to be a negative into a positive."

Although *cougar* can be a term of derision used by outsiders, it is also a badge of honor, of hard-won wisdom that challenges ageist and sexist ideas of who can have pleasure and when. The cat-as-icon never fails to rail against sexual proscriptions.

After a couple days at the AVN Expo, the specter of déjà vu materialized. The more women in cat ears and leopard prints appeared around every corner, the more I harkened back to a similar convention that was also crawling with pussy: CatCon.

At first blush it sounds like a reach. I can imagine it's even an upsetting comparison to some. There is nothing more unlike a porn convention than a cat convention. One is designed solely for adult entertainment; the other, for all ages. One is built upon love of sex; the other, love of cats. But the more I mulled it over, the more I found parallels between the two. Cat and porn devotees are simultaneously a niche and mainstream market. Who do you know that has ever had a cat? Who do you know that has ever watched porn? They are both incredibly common experiences—though some might find one or the other distasteful.

I also found a similarity in the responses I received from friends and acquaintances with whom I shared my plans to attend each event. There was a strange mix of awe and shame, excitement and aversion when I alternately said, "I'm going to a cat convention" or "I'm going to a porn convention." People have strong opinions about cats and porn—and about other people who love cats and/or porn. They are either thought to be sad and pathetic, lonely and creepy, or unequivocally cool.

The founder of CatCon, Susan Michals, knows all about what it's like to get grief for her predilections. She told the *Boston Globe* that her experience being labeled a crazy cat lady was part of the reason she started the convention. "The second I told people I had a cat, they were like, 'Oh, you're a cat lady, a crazy cat lady,'" Michals said. "It's not something to hide. I'm a cat person and proud to be a cat person."

CatCon, a celebration of all cat everything, is a reclamation of cats and cat culture—and has a particular impact for women who have been denigrated or belittled for their love of cats.

When I drove out to attend the gathering on a scorching day in August, I was greeted by regal feline faces beaming out from banners that hugged the Pasadena Convention Center. One gray longhair and one striped shorthair stared ahead, lording over the glass entrance like medieval queens. Beneath them, a trio of kittens pawed at invisible prey against a cerulean sky. Attendees in varying degrees of cat regalia poured inside, some stopping for selfies or group pictures, others craning their necks to behold the feline signage. Walking into the palatial space, I was confronted immediately with countless young women dressed as a variety of cat-girls from their favorite anime and manga. One couple walked by wearing matching "Crazy Cat Lady" and "Crazy Cat Man" shirts. Others in unassuming garb squealed as they jumped in line to behold a celebrity cat. (That cost extra.)

CatCon, like the AVN Expo, is the largest convention in its field, drawing tens of thousands of people. And, like the AVN Expo, people come out to meet their favorite celebrities, hear panel discussions about pressing issues, and, at the end of the night, party with like-minded folks. Realistically, these conventions are first and foremost driven by commerce, but there is nevertheless community that is created and built at these gatherings. These seemingly disparate conventions are unified in a similar ethos, welcoming guests of all genders in spaces dominated by women to be at home with their desires and live authentically in them without society's judgment.

As Angela White said when she took the stage to win Female Performer of the Year at the AVN awards show: "Our industry is innovative, it's progressive, and it's inclusive, and ultimately, it's important. What we do has a positive impact on people's lives."

Kayden Kross, who won the title for Best Director, offered a similar sentiment about the power of pornography and spoke out about the backlash she has faced for her work. "When I first started, I was told that porn and sex work was a weakness of character, I was told it wasn't a real job," she said in an emotional end to her acceptance speech. "My god, the resilience it takes, the confidence it takes. If you've been vulnerable, you know that the realest thing you can do is bare yourself to strangers," she opined as cheers of support erupted from the audience.

Despite virulent stigma against them in years past, cats and the women who love them have arguably emerged as the victors. Sex workers, on the other hand, have not received the same homecoming.

America's recent FOSTA-SESTA legislature signed into law in 2018 wrongfully conflates sex trafficking with sex work, making it nearly impossible for those who consensually work in the sex industry to organize, advertise, or communicate online to protect themselves. Countless sex workers, from porn performers to escorts to strippers to dommes are faced with a fast-fraying safety net that threatens their livelihoods. Even writing the word *sex* on certain digital platforms is now enough to get you shadow banned—or have your account deleted altogether. As a result, sex workers are paying the highest price.

The stigma and at times deadly consequences faced by sex workers today can be compared to the persecution that women accused of witchcraft—and sometimes their cats—encountered during the witch hunts. One, however, is a distant memory, and the other, a pressing reality.

The fear of femininity and female sexuality rooted in Christian dogma that coursed through the heart of the witch hunts has not been quelled, but has merely shifted in shape. This misogynistic discourse continues to fester and warp those enslaved by it.

Because of this rhetoric, there are distinct political undercurrents at spaces like the AVNs, and yes, even CatCon, too. It's no coincidence that women drive these events, whether as consumers or creators of content to be consumed. Although CatCon and the AVNs are no doubt enjoyed mindlessly by many, for pure pleasure's sake, these events can also serve as cultural barometers. They can inspire attendees and those watching from afar to question why we like what we like and why society says we shouldn't.

Throughout history, cats have been sluts, and sluts have been cats. And it is women who have been punished most for owning cats and owning their bodies. The way we view both speaks volumes about proscriptions against and perceptions of women and femininity.

If porn and cat conventions don't satisfy, then I offer you a more philosophical avenue to experience the fruits of the feral feminine.

Throughout researching this book, I found the "posthuman" lurking at every turn. It was in mythology and magical practices and shape-shifter fiction. It was as much a product of vibrant fantasy as it was cutting-edge science, of occult traditions and futuristic gender theory.

Posthumanism is a broad term that encompasses disparate fields and philosophies, but the meaning that applies here is shifting focus away from human subjectivity—like what philosopher Jacques Derrida attempted to do when he first met the gaze of his little cat and wondered: what does she see?

According to Pramod K. Nayar in *Posthumanism*, critical posthumanism is "the radical decentering of the traditional sovereign, coherent and autonomous human in order to demonstrate how the human is always already evolving with, constituted by and constitutive of multiple forms of life and machines."

Simply put, it means that the world doesn't turn solely for us. Humans are not the be-all and end-all, and we can learn much from nonhuman entities and intelligence that is both artificial and animal.

The feline-loving artist Leonor Fini, for example, who drew sphinxes and other figures that straddle and conjure hybrid worlds of animality and humanity, has a "posthuman sensitivity," as philosopher Francesca Ferrando suggests.

The Marx for Cats project has a similar sensibility, as G. Douglas Barrett poses in an article for *The Brooklyn Rail*. It's "located in what scholars of multiple disciplines have broadly called the posthuman turn—that odd nexus of technology, animality, possible emancipation, and possible further alienation," he explains.

Feminist scholar, spiritual activist, and writer Gloria Anzaldúa, too, fuses the possibilities of posthumanism with the shapeshifter archetype in her work. Anzaldúa's writing often references *la nahual*, Mesoamerican shape-shifters who can appear in many animal forms. Analyzing these texts, Felicity Amaya Schaeffer explains that Anzaldúa demonstrates how posthumanism isn't a technology just of the present and the future, but of the past, too.

In Anzaldúa's fiction, "cosmic world-travel is informed by Mesoamerican and pre-Aztec indigenous knowledges and practices that offer skills for traversing alien states of being and universes, skills drowned out by Western science's categorical divides across human-matter-nature," Schaeffer writes.

The posthuman is nothing new. It can be found in the traditions of Anzaldúa's ancestors and in the shape-shifting mythologies of cultures around the world. Although contemporary posthumanism often casts its eyes toward cyborgs or aliens as offering new forms of consciousness, it looks as much to animals, who have consciousness we don't have access to without the gateway of science—and, I would argue, magic.

Although most posthumanists are not concerned with and might actually be opposed to including magic as an avenue to accessing states of intelligence other than our own, I'm going to make the leap. Magic doesn't have to be anathema to science and can mean many things, from engaging in practical manifestational rituals and reading subtle clues about the world around you to interfacing with other forms of intelligence.

As Sabrina Scott explains so eloquently in *Witchbody*: "In magic, trans-species entanglement is noticed with more frequency and intensity because the agencies of other-than-humans are intentionally enlisted in collaborative efforts to do things, to effect change, to instigate material difference. Within a magical framework, entities don't exist solely to be exploited by humans."

Dozens of the practitioners I interviewed for this book expressed a similar sentiment. They emphasized how the powers of perception and intuition innate to animals—particularly cats—are aspirational attributes for their own practices. They would not be who they are without an animal to teach them patience and insight.

Through the technology of magic, and through the magic of technology, perhaps we can push past the limiting mind-sets that fix us rigidly in one place and separate us from other life-forms and other forms of intelligence. By embracing the feral feminine, which is by nature a shape-shifting designation informed equally by human and animal, we might find ways to escape gender fixity and species fixity altogether.

Xenofeminism, a relatively recent tendril of feminist thought, aligns with this approach. Described by its adherents as "a gender abolitionist, anti-naturalist, technomaterialist form of posthumanism, initiated by the working group Laboria Cuboniks," xenofeminism is expressed in continual, nimble transformations.

"Nothing should be accepted as fixed, permanent, or 'given'— neither material conditions nor social forms," states the *Xenofeminist Manifesto*.

Xenofeminists aim to question, remake, and remodel everything that orders nature and culture and what we often perceived to be immutable or unchanging like gender or reproduction. They are not the first feminists to deal in posthuman ideology, however.

Donna Haraway, who critiqued Derrida for failing to truly consider cat consciousness, is credited with furthering posthumanist philosophy with her foundational 1985 text "*A Cyborg Manifesto*." And yet, she explains in *When Species Meet* that she doesn't personally identify with the term posthuman.

"I never wanted to be posthuman, or posthumanist, any more than I wanted to be postfeminist," Haraway states. "For one thing, urgent work still remains to be done in reference to those who must inhabit the troubled categories of woman and human," she emphasizes, concluding that who she is, and her relationship with animals, is something far more elusive. "I am who I become with companion species, who and which make a mess out of categories in the making of kin and kind."

Haraway makes an important point. If we haven't perfected how to be human, can we really be past it or post it?

She may not allow us to pin her as a posthumanist—and for good reason—but it's not because she is somehow against the hybridity that the philosophy claims to embrace. The kind of ally-ship and alignment, this morphing and transforming and break-ing boundaries Haraway describes when confronted with another species, is what the feminine has undergone when faced with the feline ever since Bastet first bathed in the waters of the Nile. It is the coming together of the feral and the tamed, the human and the animal. It is why the history of cats and women, of *felininity* and femininity is more than a study in sexism. There is liberation in following this circuitous tale that can be accessed and enjoyed by anyone. It requires a curiosity, a willingness to shift shape mentally and metaphysically, while keeping the feline in mind.

This is magic we can all access. Like the reflective retinas of a cat, we can amplify what little light we are given to illuminate the possibilities that dance in the dark. We can float free like the feline clavicle, ever ready to twist fast, curl tight, leap long, or flatten at will. While under constant surveillance, we can steal the show while remaining a whisker away from authority's full control. And perhaps in looking to animality, we can steal back our humanity.

Selected Bibliography

Agrippa, Heinrich Cornelius. *Three Books of Occult Philosophy*. Macho Pubhouse, 2014.

Antelme, Ruth Schumann. *Sacred Sexuality in Ancient Egypt: The Erotic Secrets of the Forbidden Papyrus*. New York: Inner Traditions, 2001.

Archibald, Sasha. "Feline Darlings and the Anti-Cute." *Walker Reader*. September 30, 2015. *walkerart.org* Accessed July 2, 2018.

Aristotle. *The History of Animals*. Trans. D'Arcy Wentworth Thompson. The Internet Classics Archive. Web. March 1, 2018.

Asarch, Allison (allya810). "my cat is not even 1 and she's pregnant #catsaresluts #poorbabymama." March 26, 2013, 7:10 a.m. Tweet.

Atwood, Margaret. *Stone Mattress: Nine Wicked Tales*. New York: Anchor, 2015.

Bailey, Michael D. "Conrad of Marburg." *Encyclopedia of Witchcraft: The Western Tradition*. Santa Barbara, CA: ABC-CLIO, 2004.

Bain, Frederika. "Skin on Skin: Wearing Flayed Remains." *Flaying in the Pre-Modern World: Practice and Representation*. Larissa Tracy, ed. Suffolk, UK: D. S. Brewer, 2017.

Bald, Marjory A. "Jane Austen." *Women-Writers of the Nineteenth Century*. Cambridge, UK: Cambridge University Press, 1923.

Balmain, Colette. "Ghosts of Desire: Kaidan pinku eiga." *Introduction to Japanese Horror Film*. Edinburgh: Edinburgh University Press, 2008.

Barker, Jennifer M. *The Tactile Eye: Touch and the Cinematic Experience*. Berkeley, CA: University of California Press, 2009.

Barrett, G. Douglas, et al. "LOL Cats: In *Marx for Cats* the Internet Confronts Its Favorite Meme." *The Brooklyn Rail*. November 26, 2018. *brooklynrail.org* Accessed November 28, 2018.

Barrett, Michael. "Make Something Called 'Cat People,' and Make It Cheap." PopMatters. September 13, 2016. *www.popmatters.com* Accessed September 20, 2018.

Barry, Jonathan. *Witchcraft in Early Modern Europe: Studies in Culture and Belief*. Cambridge, UK: Cambridge University Press, 1998.

Batman. "Scat! Darn Catwoman." Episode 41. Directed by Oscar Rudolph. Written by Stanley Ralph Ross. ABC, January 1967.

Batman Returns. Directed by Tim Burton. Burbank, CA: Warner Bros., 1992.

Burns, William E. *Witch Hunts in Europe and America: An Encyclopedia*. Westport, CT: Greenwood Publishing Group, 2003.

Castañon, Kelsey. "Laverne Cox on Why Her Nails Are Her Biggest Power Move." September 17, 2017. *www.refinery29.com* Accessed August 7, 2018.

Cat People. Directed by Jacques Tourneur. New York: RKO Pictures, 1942.

Cat People. Directed by Paul Schrader. Universal City, CA: Universal Pictures, 1982.

Catwoman: A Celebration of 75 Years. Burbank, CA: DC Comics, 2015.

Creed, Barbara. *The Monstrous-Feminine: Film, Feminism, Psychoanalysis*. New York: Routledge, 1993.

Cummins, Dr. Alexander. "Cat Magics: The Feline in Religion, Witchcraft, and Sorcery." Lecture, Catland Books, Brooklyn, NY, July 18, 2018.

Dale, Joshua Paul, et al., eds. *The Aesthetics and Affects of Cuteness*. London: Routledge, 2016.

Darnton, Robert. *The Great Cat Massacre and Other Episodes in French Cultural History*. New York: Perseus Books, 1984.

Davisson, Zack. *Kaibyo: The Supernatural Cats of Japan*. Seattle: Chin Music Press, 2017.

de Lauretis, Teresa. *Alice Doesn't: Feminism, Semiotics, Cinema*. Bloomington, IN: Indiana UP, 1984.

Derrida, Jacques. Trans. David Wills. *The Animal That Therefore I Am*. New York: Fordham University Press, 2008.

Dijkstra, Bram. *Evil Sisters: The Threat of Female Sexuality and the Cult of Manhood*. New York: Knopf, 1996.

Dijkstra, Bram. *Idols of Perversity: Fantasies of Feminine Evil in Fin-de-Siècle Culture*. New York: Oxford University Press, 1988.

Dixon, Laurinda S. *Perilous Chastity: Women and Illness in Pre-Enlightenment Art and Medicine*. Ithaca, NY: Cornell University Press, 1995.

Driscoll, Carlos A., et al. "The Taming of the Cat." *Scientific American*. 300.6 (June 2009): 68–75.

Elizabeth, Maranda. "Trash-Magic: Signs & Rituals for the Unwanted." *Becoming Dangerous: Witchy Femmes, Queer Conjurers, and Magical Rebels*. Eds. Katie West and Jasmine Elliott. Newburyport, MA: Weiser Books, 2019.

Federici, Silvia. *Caliban and the Witch: Women, the Body, and Primitive Accumulation*. New York: Autonomedia, 2004.

Feinberg, Leslie. *Stone Butch Blues*. Ann Arbor, MI: Firebrand Books, 1993.

Fortune, Dion. *Psychic Self-Defense: The Classic Instruction Manual for Protecting Yourself against Paranormal Attack*. Newburyport, MA: Weiser Books, 2011.

Frank, Priscilla. "Pussy Power: Carolee Schneemann on the Feminist Magic of Cat Videos." *The Huffington Post*. February 18, 2016. *www.huffpost.com* Accessed October 20, 2018.

Gage, Matilda Joslyn. 1893. *Woman, Church, and State*. Reprint. Watertown, MA: Persephone Press, 1980.

Gaule, John. *Select Cases of Conscience touching Witches and Witchcraft*. 1646. The Internet Archive. Web. June 5, 2018.

Gaynor, Emily. "We Paired Fall's 6 Coolest Cat Eyes with Kittens, because Obviously." September 1, 2015. *www.teenvogue.com*. Accessed November 17, 2018.

Greene, Rosalyn. *The Magic of Shapeshifting*. York Beach, ME: Samuel Weiser, Inc., 2000.

Grew, Rachael. "Sphinxes, witches and little girls: reconsidering the female monster in the art of Leonor Fini. *Creating Humanity, Discovering Monstrosity: Myths and Metaphors of Enduring Evil*. Oxford: Inter-Disciplinary Press, 2010.

Grimassi, Raven. *The Witch's Familiar: Spiritual Partnership for Successful Magic*. Woodbury, MN: Llewellyn Worldwide, 2003.

Hall, Edith. *Aristotle's Way: How Ancient Wisdom Can Change Your Life*. London: Penguin, 2019.

Hanley, Tim. *The Many Lives of Catwoman: The Felonious History of a Feline Fatale*. Chicago: Chicago Review Press, 2017.

Haraway, Donna J. *When Species Meet*. Minneapolis: University of Minnesota Press, 2007.

Haus Frau (faeriequeenlost). "Found this kitty and am keeping it, cuz #catsaresluts they don't care who they go home with." May 10, 2013, 9:22 a.m. Tweet.

Head Banned (bb912). "#CatsAreSluts and Dogs are faithful. Best hashtag ever." March 26, 2013, 5:53 a.m. Tweet.

Heller, Tamar. "The Vampire in the House: Hysteria, Female Sexuality, and Female Knowledge in Le Fanu's 'Carmilla' (1872)." *The New Nineteenth Century: Feminist Readings of Under-read Victorian Fiction*. Eds. Barbara L. Harman & Susan Meyer. New York: Garland Publishers, 1996.

Heller, Zoe. "Book Review: Saint Joan of LA: slouching towards posterity: 'Sentimental Journeys.'" *The Independent*. January 24, 1993. *www.independent.co.uk* Accessed August 7, 2018.

Henderson, Lizanne. *Witchcraft and Folk Belief in the Age of Enlightenment: Scotland, 1670-1740*. Basingstoke, UK: Palgrave Macmillan, 2016.

Howe, Katherine, ed. *The Penguin Book of Witches*. New York: Penguin, 2014.

Howey, M. Oldfield. *The Cat in Magic, Mythology, and Religion*. New York: Crescent Books, 1989.

Hurston, Zora Neale. "Hoodoo in America." *The Journal of American Folklore*. Vol. 44, No. 174 (Oct.–Dec., 1931), pp. 317–417.

Hutton, Ronald. *The Witch: A History of Fear, from Ancient Times to the Present*. New Haven, CT: Yale University Press, 2017.

Johnson, James H. *Venice Incognito: Masks in the Serene Republic*. Berkeley, CA: University of California Press, 2017.

Kramer, Heinrich, and Jacob Sprenger. Trans. Montague Summers. *Malleus Maleficarum*. London: Arrow, 1971.

Laboria Cuboniks. *The Xenofeminist Manifesto: A Politics for Alienation*. New York: Verso, 2018.

Lahad, Kinneret. *A Table for One: A Critical Reading of Singlehood, Gender, and Time*. Manchester, UK: Manchester University Press, 2017.

Lanier, Jaron. *10 Arguments for Deleting Your Social Media Accounts Right Now*. New York: Henry Holt and Co., 2018.

Laskin, Nicholas. "Movie Review: Move over, 'John Wick': Charlize Theron does her damndest to give 'Atomic Blonde' a lethal kick of life." *Medium*. August 1, 2017. *medium.com* Accessed August 7, 2018.

Leelan, Altea (sweeetchildmine). "#CatsAreSluts. Trying to seduce you." March 26, 2013, 5:42 a.m. Tweet.

Le Fanu, Joseph Sheridan. *Carmilla*. Syracuse, NY: Syracuse University Press, 2013.

Levack, Brian P. *The Witchcraft Sourcebook*. London: Routledge, 2003.

Levi, Eliphas. Trans. Arthur Edward Waite. *Transcendental Magic: Its Doctrine and Ritual*. York Beach, ME: Weiser Books, 2001.

Lorde, Audre. *Zami: A New Spelling of My Name*. Watertown, MA: Persephone Press, 1982.

Mackay, Christopher S. *The Hammer of Witches: A Complete Translation of the Malleus Maleficarum*. Cambridge, UK: Cambridge UP, 2009.

Marx for Cats. "Election Day Special: Katzenjammer." Sunday, November 4, 2018. *vimeo.com* Accessed November 10, 2018.

McRobbie, Linda Rodriguez. "The crazy history of the 'cat lady.'" *The Boston Globe.* May 17, 2017. *www.bostonglobe.com* Accessed September 12, 2018.

Mechling, Lauren. "The 'Cat Lady' Cliche Is Over Thanks to New Feline Fashion." *The Wall Street Journal.* November 1, 2018. *www.wsj.com* Accessed October 7, 2018.

Metzler, Irina. "Witchcraft and Cats in the Middle Ages (revisited)." *Medieval Culture.* October 10, 2013. *irinametzler.org* Accessed December 5, 2018.

Molina, Laura. *Cihualyaomiquiz, the Jaguar.* Los Angeles: Insurgent Comix, 1996.

Moore, Anne Elizabeth. *Threadbare: Clothes, Sex, and Trafficking.* Portland, OR: Microcosm Publishing, 2016.

Morgan, Robin, ed. *Sisterhood Is Powerful: An Anthology of Writings from the Women's Liberation Movement.* New York: Vintage, 1970.

Mulkerrins, Jane. "Strength Becomes Her: With Angela Bassett." *Net-A-Porter.* July 20, 2018, *www.net-a-porter.com/us.* Accessed August 7, 2018.

Nayar, Pramod K. *Posthumanism.* Cambridge, UK: Polity, 2013.

Nikolajeva, Maria. "Devils, Demons, Familiars, Friends: Towards a Semiotics of Literary Cats." *Marvels & Tales.* Vol. 23, No. 2 (2009), pp. 248–67.

Obiektywie, W. "Behind 'Blackstar': An Interview with Johan Renck, the Director of David Bowie's Ten-Minute Short Film." November 19, 2015. *noisey.vice.com* Accessed April 14, 2019.

O'Meara, Radha. "Do Cats Know They Rule YouTube? Surveillance and the Pleasures of Cat Videos." *M/C Journal.* Vol. 17, No. 2 (2014).

Paulson, Ronald. *Hogarth's Harlot: Sacred Parody in Enlightenment England*. Baltimore: Johns Hopkins University Press, 2003.

Pope Gregory IX. "Vox in Rama." *World Heritage Encyclopedia*.

Redford, Donald B., ed. *The Oxford Essential Guide to Egyptian Mythology*. New York: Oxford University Press, 2002.

Roberts, Gareth. "The Descendents of Circe: Witches and Renaissance Fictions." *Witchcraft in Early Modern Europe: Studies in Culture and Belief*. Jonathan Barry et al., eds. Cambridge, UK: Cambridge University Press, 1996.

Rowling, J. K. *Harry Potter and the Prisoner of Azkaban*. New York: Arthur A. Levine Books, 1999.

Salerno, Salvatore. *Red November, Black November: Culture and Community in the Industrial Workers of the World*. Albany: State University of New York Press, 1989.

Schiff, Stacy. *The Witches: Salem, 1692*. New York: Little, Brown & Co., 2015.

Schneemann, Carolee. *Imaging Her Erotics: Essays, Interviews, Projects*. Cambridge, MA: The MIT Press, 2001.

Scot, Reginald. *The Discoverie of Witchcraft*. New York: Dover Publications, 1972.

Scott, Sabrina. "Cat's Choice Spread." *Ignota Diary 2019*. London: Ignota Books, 2019.

Scott, Sabrina. *Witchbody*. Newburyport, MA: Weiser Books, 2018.

Sollée, Kristen J. *Witches, Sluts, Feminists: Conjuring the Sex Positive*. Berkeley, CA: Stone Bridge Press, 2017.

Stewart, Harriet. "Animal Prints: Why the Perennial Trend Will Be Forever Chic." *Elle UK*. November 12, 2018. *www.elle.com/uk* Accessed November 13, 2018.

Stypczynski, Brent A. *The Modern Literary Werewolf: A Critical Study of the Mutable Motif.* Jefferson, NC: McFarland, 2013.

Syfret, Wendy. "How We Became Generation Witch." *I-D*. January 14, 2016.

The House of WTF? (TheHouseOfWTF). "Curiosity killed your virginity #CatsAreSluts." March 26, 2013, 6:31 a.m. Tweet.

Tucker, Abigail. *The Lion in the Living Room.* New York: Simon & Schuster, 2016.

Vocelle, L.A. *Revered and Reviled: A Complete History of the Domestic Cat.* Great Cat Publications, 2016.

Walker-Miekle, Kathleen. *Medieval Cats.* London: The British Library, 2011.

Wang, Ione. "A Guide to the Masks of Venice." *Culture Trip*. October 23, 2017. *theculturetrip.com* Accessed March 2, 2018.

Wee, Tommy (TommyWee). "#CatsAreSluts because they can rub up against anyone's ankles." March 26, 2013, 8:44 a.m. Tweet.

Weldon, Jo. *Fierce: The History of Leopard Print.* New York: Harper Design, 2018.

Williams, Linda Ruth. *Critical Desire: Psychoanalysis and the Literary Subject.* London: Hodder Headline, 1995.

Winick, Judd, and Guillem March. *Catwoman Volume 1: The Game.* Burbank, CA: DC Comics, 2012.

Yano, Christine R. *Pink Globalization: Hello Kitty's Trek Across the Pacific.* Durham, NC: Duke University Press, 2013.

Young, Serinity. *Women Who Fly: Goddesses, Witches, Mystics, and Other Airborne Females.* New York: Oxford University Press, 2018.

About the Author

Kristen J. Sollée is a writer, curator, and educator exploring the intersections of art, sex, and occulture. She is the founding editrix of Slutist, a sex-positive feminist website, and she lectures at The New School and across the United States and Europe. Sollée's signature college course, "The Legacy of the Witch" follows the witch through history, pop culture, and politics. Her critically-acclaimed book inspired by the course, *Witches, Sluts, Feminists: Conjuring the Sex Positive*, was published in 2017. Visit her online at *www.kristensollee.com*.

To Our Readers

Weiser Books, an imprint of Red Wheel/Weiser, publishes books across the entire spectrum of occult, esoteric, speculative, and New Age subjects. Our mission is to publish quality books that will make a difference in people's lives without advocating any one particular path or field of study. We value the integrity, originality, and depth of knowledge of our authors.

Our readers are our most important resource, and we appreciate your input, suggestions, and ideas about what you would like to see published.

Visit our website at *www.redwheelweiser.com* to learn about our upcoming books and free downloads, and be sure to go to *www.redwheelweiser.com/newsletter* to sign up for newsletters and exclusive offers.

You can also contact us at *info@rwwbooks.com* or at

Red Wheel/Weiser, LLC
65 Parker Street, Suite 7
Newburyport, MA 01950